HOW TO MOVE FROM COLLEGE INTO A SECURE JOB

HOW TO MOVE FROM COLLEGE INTO A SECURE JOB

Mary Dehner

VGM Career Horizons
a division of *NTC Publishing Group*
Lincolnwood, Illinois USA

Library of Congress Cataloging-in-Publication Data

Dehner, Mary.
    How to move from college into a secure job / Mary Dehner.

      p.   cm.
    ISBN 0-8442-4170-9
     1. Vocational guidance.   2. Job hunting.   3. College graduates—
Employment.   I. Title.
HF5381.D437
331.7′02—dc20
                                     93-4124
                                       CIP

Published by VGM Career Horizons, a division of NTC Publishing Group
4255 West Touhy Avenue
Lincolnwood (Chicago), Illinois 60646-1975, U.S.A.
© 1994 by NTC Publishing Group. All rights reserved.
No part of this book may be reproduced, stored in a retrieval system,
or transmitted in any form or by any means,
electronic, mechanical, photocopying, recording or otherwise,
without the prior permission of NTC Publishing Group.
Manufactured in the United States of America.

3 4 5 6 7 8 9 ML 9 8 7 6 5 4 3 2 1

Dedication
To my husband

Contents

Acknowledgments

Many thanks to John Yeoman, Margaret Valentine, Richard Klein, Bill Megginson, and David Robinson for their helpful comments and suggestions. Also to Carolyn J. Fausnaugh for her expert help and advice. Finally, thanks to the students in Finance at the University of Georgia who shared the triumphs and trials of their job searches with me and who let me be a part of their lives for a little while.

Introduction

Restructuring, downsizing, career plateaus, economic recession—the road to success in corporate America has changed. The threat of future unemployment has become a risk factor in every potential job. During the booming 1980s, job seekers, especially college students, had the luxury of looking for the perfect job to match their skills, while several excellent books tried to help people find the "perfect career." Today's job seekers, faced with a flatter organizational chart, must identify a core of skills they can sell to a variety of industries in a tight job market. The perfect job in the 1990s may simply be the one that pays the bills.

Getting into the job market and getting ahead in the 1990s requires company research—not only to impress the interviewer but to make sure the company will still be around in a year or two. In this aggressive job market, you must calculate three risks: your personal risk of unhappiness on the job, the economic risk posed by boom or bust cycles, and the company risk—the risk that the company will restructure and no longer require your services.

Both college students and experienced workers are confused. No one seems to have answers for those basic questions: What should I do if my fiancé wants to move to Duluth and I get an offer in Atlanta? What if I'm on academic probation? Do I really need another degree? Experienced workers, confused about making a job change, must learn to evaluate risks of future unemployment in new jobs. And everyone may need to think again about that mythical corporate ladder and decide for themselves whether the costs are worth the climb.

This book contains a company research program that will help you eliminate loser jobs. The resume section will help you quickly package your experience in a finished professional format. The interview section, based on real-life stories, will help you understand how recruiters think. The company interview section will help you evaluate a company on site and guide you through the assessment center tests.

Do You Want Fries With That?

Avoiding Minimum-Wage Risk

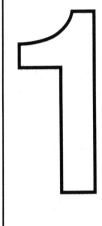

Hmmm. You're thinking, "I didn't go to college for four years to push burgers." But let's face it—without a plan you could end up right back where you were in high school, behind the counter in a polyester striped shirt. It's time to face alternatives squarely.

When your alternatives are either going to grad school or working in a fast-food restaurant and living with Mom and Dad, you need to read on. There may be something between the two extremes that is not only fun but pays well, also.

If you don't really know what you want to do, you have a lot of company. Do you need another degree? Maybe yes, maybe no. How do you find out? If your current job is giving you an ulcer, it's not too late to get another job. But first you need to figure out how risky a change will be.

In the old days, all you had to figure out was how to dress and how to interview. That has changed. Today you have to know how to protect yourself in an aggressive job market. Layoffs and downsizing put millions of experienced workers on the street during the late 1980s and the early 1990s. With no crystal ball to reveal the future, it makes sense to analyze your risks of unemployment before you take a job.

First, consider the risks lurking in every potential job. You face *personal risk* when your skills and interests don't match the job, or your personality doesn't match the people you work with. In these jobs, you probably won't do your best work, which can lead to dismissal. Next, you've got to come to grips with *economic risk,* which hits when you work in an industry that goes down hard when the economy goes down, resulting in layoffs. Finally, *company risk* increases your chances of future unemployment if the company you work for routinely trims labor expenses to appear more profitable to investors, which could mean either layoffs or 14-hour days due to reduced staff.

In a perfect world, the higher your risk of unemployment, the more money you would expect to receive. Certainly, if you were investing in a risky project, you might lose all your money in the investment. Employment risk should work the same way. Unfortunately, it works that way only for top executives. CEOs of large companies can insure their income against unemployment by demanding "golden parachute" clauses in their contracts which guarantee a certain amount of money if they get fired. Since the rest of us don't get such benefits, we need to devise our own strategies for reducing our risk of unemployment before we even accept the job.

Tune Out Mom and Dad: Personal Risk

When you are desperately unhappy in your job, you face the personal risk of unemployment. Perhaps you were forced into the job by well-intentioned relatives, or perhaps you fell into it because you didn't know what you wanted to do with your life. Now you feel stuck.

If you are just graduating from college and evaluating your options, be wary of those who would force you into uncomfortable positions. How often have you let yourself be influenced by these do-gooders' words of advice?

- *But my parents say I should . . .*
- *But my husband/wife really thinks I should . . .*
- *But my teachers always pushed me to . . .*

Face it. Are they going to do the job eight hours a day? So what if your parents are paying the bills? So what if your spouse wants you in a certain industry? So what if your father-in-law says the best entrée into business is through his company?

Do what you want to do—period. No one owns you. If people want to control you by offering you money for school only if you do what they want, calmly tell them you must find a career that feels right for you. You appreciate their generosity, but you must make your own choices. Accept the responsibility for winning or losing. Just make it your own choice.

No two people have the same goals or needs. Some people are goal setters; others go on intuition and gut feelings. Don't be intimidated by what others do. There is no "right" career path. What you choose depends on what is important to you.

What's So Hot About Ambition?

Every day, students come into my office with ambitious plans. They want to move ahead, be recognized, and become powerful. There's nothing wrong with having ambition, but at what cost do they purchase this success? And is it really success? Too often people tie their own sense of identity too closely to what they hope people will think about them. They get lost in the "I must impress the world" shuffle. Here's a different perspective:

To succeed as a human being:

You don't have to climb any ladders;
You don't have to earn recognition or awards;
You don't have to be a leader;
You don't have to be aggressive;
You don't have to be a phony;
You don't have to prove anything to family, strangers, or potential mates.
But you do have to impress your boss or potential bosses because they control your income.

Ultimately, the only thing you need to do to be successful is earn enough money to support yourself and your family (if you have one) and live your life the best you can. As you gain more skills, you may want to advance and do something new because you are intellectually curious and have energy.

The old ladder-climbing style of advancement popular in big companies from the end of World War II through the 1980s has disappeared because the ladder rungs have disappeared. Climbing ladders today looks more like a zigzag climb from company to company every couple of years.

Driven less by a need to impress the world than by a need to sustain and increase income, the zigzag climber:

- maintains and increases income to outpace inflation (raises are bigger when you change companies);

- maintains job security by keeping skills up to date;

- keeps his or her mind alert by learning new things.

Whom do you want to impress? The people who can pay you more money. They have the sackful of pay raises and new responsibilities that will help you become more marketable, which ultimately gives you more choices and more job security. And that's the reason to advance: to have more fun or more choices—not to show the folks back home that you can do it.

You don't have to prove to your dad that you are smart and successful. You don't have to make up for his mistakes. You don't have to be an actor because Mom always wanted to be one. And you don't have to be happy all the time.

A little discontent is normal. No job will make you happy all the time, but you might think it should if you have been fed the myth that all jobs should always be totally fulfilling. The myth may have come to you from a job-search book, or it may have taken root in the lonely times that you sat in your room as a child when things weren't going well at home. Did you ever imagine Mom and Dad would have been happier at home if they had been happier at work? How often did you see your father slumped in a chair, staring into space because he was unhappy at the office? Or how about Mom? Was she unhappy in her work or role? It's comforting to think that if only they had gotten enough education or a job that let them spread their wings and use their skills, they would have been happy. And so the thinking goes; we all would have had happier home lives as children if Mom and Dad had been fulfilled. While there may be a grain of truth here, it's certainly not the entire answer.

While a bad boss, unreasonable pressure, long hours for low pay, and lack of recognition can be disappointing and motivate you to look elsewhere, work is still only one part of your life. The other roles you play—friend, parent, lover, volunteer, amateur football player—are equally important. During the 1980s, people forgot about these other parts of themselves and became enamored with the world of work. They bragged about their long hours. It was chic to be married to one's job. Then the slash-and-burn restructuring of the late 1980s eliminated many of those demanding jobs, and those hard-working baby boomers were left with a bitter memory of the nights devoted to the company.

The plain truth is that work doesn't make you happy or unhappy. It doesn't make you a worthwhile person or a worthless person. Don't allow your entire being to be defined by a job someone is paying you to do. At some point you may not be doing that work anymore. Then what happens to your self-esteem? Do you suddenly become a worthless person if the company "restructures" and puts you back on the street? Of course not.

Yet even if you don't extract your entire sense of self-worth from a job, and even if you have realistic expectations about happiness, you will find jobs that you abhor. That's why you need to know what your personal risk aversions are. For some, it will be excess supervision (the feeling that someone is breathing down your neck). For others it will be inadequate standards and rewards, or an office full of smokers and gossips—or the thought of having to stay indoors every day for eight hours. Researching yourself to nail down your more serious aversions and preferences can improve your odds of getting a job you can keep for a few years.

The risk of personal unhappiness to watch out for is either a gross mismatch between your skills and those needed for the job or a poor fit between you and your work environment (i.e., the rules and/or people make you crazy). These personal risk factors reduce job security because you will not work well when you are not yourself, and not doing good work could lead to termination.

Your first job out of school won't determine your entire life's course. If you have made it through college, you probably have more opportunities than your parents and grandparents had. You may feel that there is no excuse for not finding the perfect career. Then you'll be happy, right? Maybe, but maybe not. For example, can you say that you are happy right now, this very minute? If the answer is yes (for whatever reason), my guess is that you will be happy in life. Already you are either happy or unhappy, and you haven't even embarked on a career yet.

Can work be fun? Sure. Will it be fun all the time? No. You'll know you face the personal risk of unhappiness when you begin to dread going to work every morning. When things are going well, however, you will feel a little bubble of enthusiasm and fun every once in a while. You'll have a chance to learn something new, and facing work every day will offer something you want—not something you dread.

Hedging Economic Risk

Today's job market calls for flexibility. That means identifying as many of your own skills as possible to qualify yourself for as many different jobs as possible. That way, when one segment of the economy threatens your job security, you have other alternatives to keep income coming in (besides working at a fast food restaurant). Think of your career as you might think of a stock portfolio. You don't want all your money tied up in one stock; if something happens to that stock, your whole portfolio goes down the tubes. The same is true with your talent. Diversify. If you have your entire identity and experience tied to one industry or one company, you may have too much faith in that business.

Companies are changing the way they do business. Specialists are less in demand since so many companies have switched to self-directed work teams. These teams take the place of many levels of managers. Hourly workers in team companies now do their own production planning, scheduling, and quality assurance.

These changes to self-directed work teams will not be limited to manufacturing. The team concept may invade business at all levels in the coming decade as companies recognize that employees are in the best position to make decisions. This method also cuts supervisory labor costs substantially. Several layers of management will be gone. Those who remain will be coaches and resource people for the workers.

To diversify in this new environment, identify a core of marketable skills. Then look at the different jobs that require a piece of that core. That way you can wear different hats on different teams at different companies. If you are a writer, for example, get your feet wet in journalism, public relations, teaching, marketing, or book publishing. If you are in accounting or finance, work for a few years in a public accounting firm, a few in a specialized area in a company, and a few in a private consulting firm. Try to figure out what skills are in demand, and stick your nose in that area of the business to learn it. In short, become a generalist while honing your best skills.

Could you see yourself, for example, in such different roles as a production manager for a plant and as director of human resources? Could you see yourself in sales or in finance? You increase your flexibility if you get experience in both the support and line functions of a company. But getting locked into only support functions such as human resources or public relations can also keep you trapped at lower levels of the corporate echelon. Employees who work in a company's core business areas, such as marketing, production, and sales, are more likely to be promoted, according to a recent employment study. And even if you are not game for ladder climbing, you increase your odds of getting another job if you have had a few years of experience in different areas.

The worst jobs pay little and extract much. If the job is a high-stress, low-paying job but is only temporary, you may be able to put up with the unpleasantness for a while. But take the job only if you are starving and have to pay the rent, or if you can gain a skill quickly to sell elsewhere. If the job does not offer you a chance to learn something new that you can sell either within the company at another level or outside the company, think twice. These jobs force you to focus on a sliver of the business, their business, without letting you diversify by developing skills in several areas.

If you decide against being a skilled generalist and focus instead on one skill, you may get a very high return on your time and energy investment—or you may not. It's a high-risk gamble. You may become the best linguistics professor in the world, but that won't save you if every university with a linguistics department decides to cut the department because not enough students are enrolled. Or, after gaining moderate success as a rock musician, your star could fade, and you might end up pumping gas.

If you want to get one career and stick with it all the way through, you may be able to make more money, but your flexibility may be limited. If at some point you decide to change careers, it will be a very big change, and there's no guarantee an employer will want to take a chance on an older employee with no experience in the new area.

Doing one thing and one thing very well was the slogan of Kentucky Fried Chicken a few years ago. Whatever happened to that idea? Look at fast-food menus today. They hardly ever focus on one thing. Now you get everything from a breakfast burrito to a multi-course meal at fast-food restaurants. Doing one thing well works only if you can differentiate yourself from all of the competition. If you have the talent to compete in the Olympics of life, go for it. But having a back-up source of income isn't such a bad idea, either.

Now let's look at the ultimate unhedged employment risk: marriage without a financial net. College students these days generally know better than to get married and quit working. Developing no marketable job skills while relying completely on one income of one person doing one thing courts significant economic risk. Aside from the risk of divorce, which substantially reduces income, this arrangement ties two people to one industry. If the industry declines, not one but two people are on the street—one with no skills and one with skills that relate to a dead industry. Are there exceptions? Sure. And there are certainly justifiable reasons for choosing such an arrangement, such as child care. But the economic risk of this arrangement is also worth considering.

There's no perfect hedge for unemployment risk due to economic downturns, but becoming enough of an expert on a subject to sell your knowledge and services to more than one market is another excellent way to hedge your risk of unemployment. Don't underrate your potential for developing this expertise. Often, it just means keeping your ears open, accepting lower pay while you learn your craft, and then selling your knowledge to someone else. For example, the next time someone says there's an opportunity for you to do something new, but it doesn't pay much money, don't tune out. Most "first" jobs start out very small, carry relatively low prestige, and pay poorly. But good first jobs can give you a chance to learn something new that you can sell somewhere else for a higher price.

My first job was as a fund-raiser for extremely low pay at a small Christian college; no one was impressed when I took the job. But it was a job. I learned my craft and eventually sold my new knowledge to several clients as a consultant. I realized that I liked writing more than fund raising, so later I took a job as a stringer for a newspaper. The pay was about $20 to $25 a story. Considering it took me about 12 hours to write a story the first few times I got an assignment, I was making about what a baby-sitter makes ($2.08 per hour), and that was on a good day. The woman who told me about the job said she wasn't interested in it because it wouldn't pay enough for the time she would have to put in. Later, as I became more experienced, it took only an hour to produce a story, which boosted my hourly rate. All the while, I learned my trade. The newspaper eventually hired me as a reporter and assistant editor. In effect, I sold my skills to the newspaper, which paid me lower wages while I apprenticed.

Your range of experience includes what you do on your off-hours too. If you like working on cars in your spare time, you can leverage this skill in economic downtimes—but only if you let people who could potentially hire you know that you do good work. Quietly working on a project requiring skill and never telling anyone about it does not improve your risk profile. But joining a club of enthusiasts, such as a sports car club filled with members who need your advice on their carburetors, helps protect you from the risk of unemployment. First, as a result of joining the club, you have a network of people who can be on the look-out for a job for you. Second, you may be able to pick up work to keep income coming in while you look. Third, the quality of work you do may impress people and make them want to hire you in another capacity.

The multiple-skills approach is one way to reduce economic employment risk, but what if your company suddenly decides to downsize? Where does that put you?

Company Risk   Job cutting may well become the theme of the lean and mean 1990s. Sears, Roebuck & Co. trimmed 40,500 jobs between 1990 and 1992, and then in 1992 announced plans to cut an additional 2,000 workers. It cut experienced sales staff in appliances and furniture and replaced them with lower-paid clerks. So much for company loyalty.

IBM cut 20,000 jobs in 1991. The cutbacks and reorganization were intended to make the company more efficient and better able to react to the international market by placing more responsibility in fewer hands. Cutbacks reduce costs, which increases profits, which in turn makes the stock attractive to more investors—or so the thinking goes.

So how do you tell whether your company is going to go on a job-cutting binge? That's not an easy question. And it's especially tough to tell when you are going into your first job. In the research chapters, we will present a basic approach to analyzing a company and its position in the competitive market. Companies with many years of low or no growth opportunities, sagging sales, and high debt may cut costs by cleaning house. If they have four times more employees than their closest competitor, shareholders may demand changes that boost earnings. Or, in the event of a takeover, the weak divisions of a conglomerate could be spun off and sold to pay for the acquisition. In any case, you could be looking for a job again sooner than you want to.

General Electric downsized its workforce in the late 1980s. With its smaller workforce, the company says it wants its managers to have more responsibility. What it doesn't say is that these energetic managers are often doing the work ten employees did before the cutbacks. The morale of the workforce is rarely figured into stock prices. Employee discontent becomes an issue only when the employees unionize and strike, and that rarely happens in white-collar jobs. Looking for clues of employee discontent is part of your research we will explore in Chapter 9 on interviews.

Your risks of future unemployment—personal risk of unhappiness, economic risk, and company risk—sound discouraging and make employment seem dangerous. But risk is not dangerous unless you close your eyes to it. Every time you cross a street or pull up to a stop sign in your car, you face the risk that another motorist will not obey the stop sign and ram you as you enter the intersection. That ever-present risk doesn't stop you from getting in your car and driving across town. You know it's there, and you account for it by looking around you when you pull up to the stop. You wouldn't ignore risk by driving blind.

In your job search, no one has ever told you the risks and pitfalls. No one ever told you how to avoid them. Without evaluating them, you would be driving blind into your career. Understanding yourself and doing a small bit of focused homework on your potential job, the company, and its philosophy, finances, and preferences significantly reduces your risks. And yes, you can be happy, really delighted with work when it fits your skills and pays you enough to suit your lifestyle.

Getting Started Will Calm Your Jangled Nerves

You may be feeling stressed out or not in control because suddenly you feel your life is in front of you instead of being on hold until you hit the next exam. But your life wasn't really on hold while you were in school. Your life is never on hold. You are always thinking, making choices, and figuring things out no matter where you are. Work does require more of that effort, since few jobs come with instructions, but thinking about your life is a continuous process.

When you work for pay, no one prods you to stay on the task (unless you are working for minimum wages). No one gives you grades every quarter to let you know how you are doing. When you go to work, you suddenly begin measuring your own progress, setting your own standards, and developing a sense of pride in what you do, even when no one praises your achievements. You take charge, not your teachers, and your job search is the first phase of that process.

The lack of structure and regular rewards in the work world can be scary. Some people cope with this by seeking jobs that require extensive training in order to keep the passive feeling of being told what to do. Others stay in school because they are afraid to make career choices or because they assume no one will want to hire them. If that's the approach you prefer, go ahead and take things at your own speed. There are no right or wrong decisions to make at this point. But think about why you are making those choices. What are you afraid of? Remember, you know as much as the next person—maybe more.

If you have read this far, you probably have initiative. No matter what job you get, you will need initiative. That's the stuff that will help you succeed in whatever you try to do. Taking initiative means leading yourself. You don't have to lead other people to have initiative; you just have to be able to look around and figure things out for yourself. Right now anxiety can eat at you—especially when the clock is ticking, and you don't know how to get started. Every day you put off thinking about looking for a job, your anxiety increases. Maybe you are drinking a little more, sleeping more, partying more—anything to avoid thinking about doing what you are scared to do.

Getting started can relieve that anxiety. Suddenly, looking for a job is not a big black box that you fear opening. Instead, it's a phone call here, a trip to the library there, and one, two, maybe twenty interviews. The more you take control of your job search, the more relaxed you will feel and the more productive you will be.

But What If I Screw Up?

That's always a possibility, no matter who is paying the bills. But this is the time in your life when you are supposed to make mistakes. They cost less now than they will later. You can do just about whatever you want until you are 30. Your goal right now is to get a job.

If you have a family to support, you have to determine

how much a change will affect your personal happiness risk and how that affects your family. If you are desperately unhappy now, you are already at risk. You probably aren't doing your best at work, and you may be too stressed out to be your best with the people you love. In the coming chapters, you will be able to evaluate where you are and how serious the risks in a new job will be.

What If I'm on Academic Probation?

Unfortunately, to find a good job you are going to have to buckle down and make the grades. Yes, it's true; recruiters do screen out job applicants who have less than a B average (3.0 grade point average on a 4.0 scale). Don't despair if you have a lower grade point average; there are ways around this. But if you are still in school, throw as much energy into your studies as you can because the grades you get now can haunt you for a long time. Though most employers beyond your first one won't look at your transcript, a few nitpickers will. Just think about having to explain away your D's to several different interviewers over your lifetime. It will be a lot easier to say, "Yes, I screwed up, but I brought my grade point average back to 3.0 by senior year when I finally settled down."

In most jobs, you want to show the world what you can do by getting a sterling recommendation from your employer. That means doing everything the employer wants and more (unless he or she asks you to do something illegal).

It means having a cooperative and volunteering attitude. It means building your reputation in a way that will ultimately do more for you than grades or degrees from prestigious schools (though don't discount the importance of either one of these career boosters). If your first job is not the perfect job, you will get a better one next year. There really are no perfect jobs.

Would You Rather Crunch Numbers or Cook Pasta?

Researching Yourself

One of my former students, Brenda, had strong quantitative skills. She excelled in finance, but she also had a flair for fashion. I should have been listening more carefully when she told me her career plans. She said she was going into banking because she liked people. Yet the jobs she interviewed for in commercial lending would initially place her far from people in a back office where she would analyze credit reports. It didn't occur to me right away how "peopleless" her job would be. After one year, she called me. She was climbing the walls.

"I spend all day in a tiny office at the bank crunching numbers. I never see anyone; I never pictured banking like this," she told me on the phone. "I want a job where I'll see people and travel."

When she had interviewed for the job, she had never asked what she would really be doing on the job. She just assumed it would give her what she wanted. And she didn't know what she wanted until she realized her job didn't have it. Brenda, like many students, had envisioned her job at the bank as a scaled-down version of "L.A. Law." What people would actually *do* between buzzing up on the mirrored elevator in the morning and buzzing off for power lunches was a bit hazy.

After thinking about her interests and abilities, she decided to look for a career in the fashion industry. But did she make the right choice in quitting her job to find the job of her dreams? Some career counselors would say yes. I say maybe. She may have just needed a transfer to a more people-oriented job at the bank.

It's true. No job is fun all of the time, but a good balance helps you avoid the trap of getting a job that requires you to do things you hate 90 percent of the time and things you love 10 percent of the time. As Richard Nelson Bolles points out in his valuable job-search book, *What Color Is Your Parachute?,* you will be happier if you do something you enjoy doing.

Every job calls for certain skills. I was a newspaper reporter in the Chicago suburbs before my husband was transferred to another city. When we got settled in our new home, my first career move was naturally to find another newspaper job. The only job available at the local paper was a copy editing job, where I worked as a temporary replacement for the copy editor on maternity leave. Since I hadn't really thought things through, and the job was in the same industry, I figured it was a good career move. I was wrong. I hadn't really matched my skills to the job.

If I had compared my skills with the primary requirements for the copy editing job, I wouldn't have taken it. I had forgotten how sharply copy editing differs from writing. It's a nitpicky business that requires good interpersonal skills, especially when you have to rewrite front-page stories and face the icy stares of angry reporters. Copy editors typically use *comparing* skills with data, *serving* skills with people, and *handling* skills with things. (These skills will be explained more fully in this chapter as you uncover your special talents in the exercises that follow.) Copy editors also lay out pages, which requires *setting up* skills. My skills are in writing and researching (*synthesizing* and *analyzing*) and not in editing (though I developed a healthy respect for copy editors after fighting editing battles). This is not to say that you can't grow with a job and develop a new set of skills. Growing is healthy. But selecting a job that is diametrically opposed to your fundamental skills can lead to frustration.

Another friend of mine went to Harvard for his M.B.A.

He graduated in time to jump into the investment banking craze of the 1980s. Though he had the brains and the analytical ability to put merger and acquisition deals together, he was missing the fundamental skills to make it all work—sales skills (*persuading* and *negotiating*). He eventually discovered that he would rather do the analytical work than get on the phone and sell the deals. He decided to go back to school to get a Ph.D. and teach finance. He found a career that required analytical ability and that didn't require sales skills.

The Work You Do

The work you ultimately do should be something you are fairly good at or have the potential to be good at. It may not relate to anything you learned in school; your best skills may be those you developed years ago. For example, were you the one who always settled the fights on the playground when you were a kid? If so, you may want a job that allows you to use negotiating skills.

What if your favorite skills are pitching a fast ball or crocheting afghans? Does that mean you should try out for the major leagues or start your own cottage industry? Heavens no—not unless you have major league talent or entrepreneurial skills. We are talking about *realistic* career goals in this book. The question we need to ask is this: What does your love for pitching fast balls say about you? Does it mean you like teamwork or that you like to work alone? Does it mean you like the outdoors or being a coach? Each of these likes and dislikes may be part of one of your marketable skills.

The same goes for crocheting afghans. Is it the precision handwork you like? How about working alone or having control over a project? Is it creativity that's important? The skills you enjoy using most may not be the skills that you will use to earn a living, but if you can put together a career that gives you whatever it is you want (money, creativity, teamwork, the outdoors—the list depends on you), you will probably enjoy yourself more and be more successful.

Go with what you are good at. Don't try to force yourself into a career at which you will never succeed. Though this sounds obvious, the truth is that you probably won't do well at sales if you don't like selling. I hear you saying, "But I've never tried, maybe I would *like* selling!" In that case, get a summer job selling encyclopedias or vacuum cleaners, and if you still like it, then go for it.

Why You Need Research

Here's an example of what you *don't* want to happen when you interview for a job.

> *Interviewer:* "What do you offer the company?"
>
> *Student:* "Huh?"

The student stared at the ceiling for awhile and finally pointed out that he is punctual. Since he couldn't identify his skills on the spot, he didn't get the job.

Therefore, know your skills to avoid the flat-out embarrassment that comes from being caught off guard in an interview. Instead of stuttering or staring at the ceiling, you want to calmly discuss your strong points and give an example or two to illustrate them.

Match Your Skills to Job Requirements

Most students are quick to point out that they have good interpersonal skills, and some say they have good computer skills. Few, however, have actual examples of those skills, which makes for weak credibility in a job interview. Imagine that the following job description was made available before an interview. (This is an excerpt from an actual job description sent to the University of Georgia by a recruiter.)

TITLE: Management Associate

ORGANIZATIONAL RELATIONSHIP:
Reports to: Manager
Supervises: None

GENERAL FUNCTION: Preparation to assume management position requiring skills in sales, management operations, and credit.

MAJOR SKILLS AND REQUIREMENTS:
4-year college degree
sales skills
organizational skills
negotiation skills
analytical ability
excellent speaking and writing skills
self-discipline
initiative
human relations skills
completion of basic accounting course within six
   months
ability to be flexible in changing work environment

If you were interviewing for this job, would you have examples of your organizational skills, negotiation skills, and initiative? If not, unless you are extremely quick at thinking on your feet, you would stare at the ceiling like our punctual young man. My students tend to get jobs when they use what I call stories of achievement, which are simply brief examples of when they used a particular skill and the result.

Stories of achievement include:

- What you did.

- How you did it.

- The result.

Here's an example:

What you did: Set up a collection program for fraternity fees that were past due.

How you did it: Devised spread sheet, asked for input, presented it to the group.

The result: Improved collections with no hard feelings.

What it shows: Initiative, good interpersonal skills, follow-through, results.

Identifying Your Skills

Use this list to identify your strengths and to match your abilities with potential jobs. This is your raw material for interviewing. The list comes from the *Dictionary of Occupational Titles,* a reference published by the U.S. Department of Labor that identifies more than 10,000 jobs and the skills required to do them. The book is available at many libraries.

Directions: Mark the skills you enjoy using. Jot down an example of what you were doing when you were using the skill and what the result was. Also explain how you did it.

Information Skills

(0) Synthesizing.

☐ ☐ ☐
like so-so dislike

Can you think of an example of a time when you had to summarize
something, make a plan, or evaluate different options?
"In our 1993 student government, I evaluated two plans for allocating
student activity fees, and wrote up my recommendation. The result: The
plan was adopted and student groups and administration agreed it resulted
in fairer funding for all groups." (To use this in a job interview, also explain
how you did it, such as: listed pros and cons, interviewed student groups
on needs, etc. Consider what you liked about doing this.)

What I did; how I did it; why I liked it; the result.

_____

_____

_____

_____

(1) Coordinating.

☐ ☐ ☐
like so-so dislike

Have you ever had to organize something that involved other people?
"Organized a softball team for intramurals of people who previously
considered themselves 'nonathletes.' Result: It was the first time they
experienced team play. Won 6 out of 12 games." (Also explain how you did
it. Did you use persuasion? Planning? Coaching skills? Coordinating is a
major part of many jobs. This is evidence you can do it.)

What I did; how I did it; why I liked it; the result.

_____

_____

_____

_____

(2) Analyzing.

☐ ☐ ☐
like   so-so dislike

Have you ever had to sit down and figure out how and why something happens? Did you ever have to pick things apart, piece by piece, either physically or mentally?

"Analyzed why my car wasn't working. Tested coil, wiring, fuses. The result: I fixed the car and saved $100." (Did you like doing it? This skill shows you have the patience and logic to solve problems. You also may have done well in logic classes such as calculus or using computer software to solve problems. If you like analyzing things, look for jobs that have an analytical component.)

What I did; how I did it; why I liked it; the result.

_____

_____

_____

_____

(3) Compiling.

☐ ☐ ☐
like   so-so dislike

Have you ever had to put things in order?

"While working at summer job, put together information from several different files to compile a report for my boss. Organized files by category. Result: created a new report that told sales representatives how effectively company was selling in various geographic areas and product lines. Further result: new sales efforts could then be directed in that area."

What I did; how I did it; why I liked it; the result.

_____

_____

_____

_____

(4) Computing.
☐ ☐ ☐
like   so-so dislike

How do you feel about working with numbers?
  "Calculated costs for installing a new kitchen in sorority house.
Computed cash outlays and maintenance cost. As a result, data provided a
realistic estimate of costs." Or, "I always balance my checkbook because I
like to know exactly where I stand." (These are signs of computing skills.
Do you like the part of math that calls for calculating?)

What I did; how I did it; why I liked it; the result.

_____

_____

_____

_____

(5) Copying, storing, retrieving.
☐ ☐ ☐
like   so-so dislike

Have you ever had to file or organize information so that you could find it
again later?
  "Reorganized filing system while working part-time in doctor's office.
Redesigned system to be numerical by Social Security number and
cross-referenced by family name. Result: increased efficiency (saved 3
minutes on each retrieval) and receptionists no longer kept patients waiting
while files were being retrieved."

What I did; how I did it; why I liked it; the result.

_____

_____

_____

_____

(6) Comparing.

☐ ☐ ☐
like   so-so dislike

Do you like to comparison-shop to find an item at the best price for the money? How about comparing work that has been done against a standard of how it is supposed to be done?

"Compared data entered in computer to work orders. Able to find errors faster than other workers. How I did it: made template of standard entry form, compared each entry by grouping on entry form instead of individually. Additional skills: attention to detail. The result: cut time of checking by six minutes per load, which resulted in less downtime in the company and speedier shipment of product to customers."

What I did; how I did it; why I liked it; the result.

_____

_____

_____

_____

People Skills

(0) Mentoring.

☐ ☐ ☐
like so-so dislike

Have you ever taken someone under your wing? How about coaching, advising, or motivating people? Did you ever act as a consultant?

"Coached little league team. Worked on developing teamwork and skills. Succeeded in motivating team to work together. Team won championship." (How did you approach the task? What did you do that helped make them winners? Could you use the same skills in motivating employees? Picture the mentoring skill as the top skill in the people section. Now visualize a head chef at a four-star restaurant who takes apprentice chefs under his or her wing. The chef will be a mentor and also an instructor, supervisor, planner, creator, and negotiator. The chef will have good organizational skills and good attention to detail.)

What I did; how I did it; why I liked it; the result.

_____

_____

_____

_____

(1) Negotiating.

☐ ☐ ☐
like so-so dislike

Have you ever had to be the peacemaker, see two different sides?

"Negotiated dispute at sorority between two committees. Helped each air grievances, found common ground. Result: Work was more evenly divided and morale improved. Evidence of improved morale: better attendance at committee meeting, more volunteers for committees." (Are you the person people turn to to resolve disputes? Would you like to do more of this and get paid for it?

What I did; how I did it; why I liked it; the result.

_____

_____

_____

_____

(2) Instructing.

☐ ☐ ☐

like   so-so dislike

Have you ever taught someone something?

   "Tutored foreign students in English. Set goals, determined individual needs. Result: six of ten students' grades in English improved from D's to A's." (Was it fun? Did this give you a sense of fulfillment? Instructing is not limited to jobs in education. There's a growing market for trainers in industry.)

What I did; how I did it; why I liked it; the result.

_____

_____

_____

_____

(3) Supervising.

☐ ☐ ☐

like   so-so dislike

Have you ever had to monitor someone else's performance?

   "Supervised night shift at Pizza World. Set schedules, resolved disputes, promoted good morale through regular communication. Result: absenteeism reduced by 50 percent. Further result: higher profits for company due to stability of employees and less downtime due to training." (Did you like this role? Did your employees appreciate your management style? Natural skills at management might be an important component of a future job. On the other hand, if you were thrown into a supervisory job without any training and had a negative experience, don't give up on the idea of being a supervisor; you just might need more experience and training in this area.)

What I did; how I did it; why I liked it; the result.

_____

_____

_____

_____

(4) Diverting.

☐ ☐ ☐
like   so-so dislike

Do you like to tell stories or jokes or perform?

"Performed in campus plays. Managed time to maintain grades during rigorous rehearsal schedule. The result: maintained B average and performances were favorably reviewed by press." (Other skills you may have developed in the process include taking direction gracefully, working under pressure, and learning how to put yourself in someone else's shoes.)

What I did; how I did it; why I liked it; the result.

_____

_____

_____

_____

(5) Persuading.

☐ ☐ ☐
like   so-so dislike

Have you ever sold someone on an idea or a product? Have you ever convinced people to do things your way?

"Sold newspaper subscriptions door-to-door. Planned nightly route to cover entire sector of city. Was persistent in face of rejection. Was sensitive to needs of potential customers. Result: sold more subscriptions than any other salesperson on that route during that summer." (These are strong components of sales jobs: persistence, listening, and planning can make for a successful career. Did you enjoy it? Selling doesn't have to be door-to-door. In every job, you use persuasive skills every time you have to convince your co-workers or superiors of your ideas or viewpoints.

What I did; how I did it; why I liked it; the result.

_____

_____

_____

_____

(6) Speaking/Signaling.

☐ ☐ ☐
like   so-so dislike

Do you like to write, speak, or interview people?
"Interviewed campus officials for newspaper article on racism. Researched topic, planned interview questions, wrote story. Result: article won an award for reporting" or "article credited for changing campus policies." (Do you enjoy communicating with people and then translating what they say for another medium? You might enjoy journalism, teaching, counseling, public relations, or any of the communications professions.)

What I did; how I did it; why I liked it; the result.

_____

_____

_____

_____

(7) Serving.

☐ ☐ ☐
like   so-so dislike

Have you ever taken care of someone who was sick or waited on someone in a restaurant?
"Waited on customers at family restaurant. Focused on speed of delivering orders and friendliness. Result: earned $200 per night in tips. Normal tips are only $50 per night." (Jobs that call for serving skills are not limited to restaurants. Customer service in all professions is a growing industry. Companies want people who can empathize with customers and meet their needs.)

What I did; how I did it; why I liked it; the result.

_____

_____

_____

_____

(8) Taking instructions.   ☐ ☐ ☐

like   so-so dislike

Can you think of an example of a time when you had to follow instructions?
    "Took directions and followed through on complicated new computer software program. Listened attentively, took notes, practiced. Result: able to execute program in less than half the normal time." (Where would the astronauts be if they couldn't follow directions? This is no small thing, and being skilled and quick at learning new things is a valuable skill in any job.)

What I did; how I did it; why I liked it; the result.

_____

_____

_____

_____

Skills with Things

(0) Setting up.

☐ ☐ ☐
like   so-so   dislike

Have you ever set up a display or machinery?

"Set up display of food products at grocery store, following manufacturer's layout. Created eye-catching display that resulted in 10 percent increased sales of product." (Setting up can be an important skill in everything from retail to art museums to industrial production. If you are good at it, look for evidence and for a job that requires it.)

What I did; how I did it; why I liked it; the result.

_____

_____

_____

_____

(1) Precision work.

☐ ☐ ☐
like   so-so   dislike

Have you ever done precision handwork?

"Operated a drill press at factory to produce steel product. Attended to detail; best quality control record on floor." (If you can do precision work with few errors, you probably have good attention to detail. This is a valuable skill in everything from accounting to designing computer programs, or from fine craft work to precision industrial production.)

What I did; how I did it; why I liked it; the result.

_____

_____

_____

_____

(2) Operating/Controlling.

☐ ☐ ☐
like so-so dislike

Have you ever operated machinery?

"Operated labeler at factory. Monitored machine to make sure it was printing properly. Learned to fix minor problems in order to keep the machine running and production moving, resulting in less downtime for the production line." (To do this effectively, you would have to analyze what was wrong and stay on top of the job—an important skill and a possible indicator of mechanical ability.)

What I did; how I did it; why I liked it; the result.

_____

_____

_____

_____

(3) Driving/Operating.

☐ ☐ ☐
like so-so dislike

How do you feel about driving and operating vehicles—anything from delivery cars to heavy equipment?

"Drove forklift at carpet mill. Raw material consistently delivered on time; no lost time due to accidents. (Did you learn to operate the equipment quickly and efficiently? No lost time indicates mastery over the machine and good judgment.)

What I did; how I did it; why I liked it; the result.

_____

_____

_____

_____

(4) Manipulating.

☐ ☐ ☐
like so-so dislike

Working with hand tools or machines: knitting, carving wood, weaving, painting—how do you like it?

"Knitted afghans for family. Set daily goals for completion of project. Attentive to detail and correcting for errors. Like working with hands. Produced three afghans in less than four months to use as Christmas gifts." (Shows planning, detail, creativity, patience and persistence, as well as ability to meet goals.)

What I did; how I did it; why I liked it; the result.

_____

_____

_____

_____

(5) Tending.

☐ ☐ ☐
like so-so dislike

Have you ever worked in a factory or in any job in which you had to watch a machine function, stopping it or adjusting it as needed?

"Ran deep fryer at McDonalds. Monitored orders, kept machine frying. Result: reduced customer waiting time for orders by 12 percent and promoted better feelings among employees in stressful work environment." (Shows efficiency, ability to maintain production in stressful environment, teamwork.)

What I did; how I did it; why I liked it; the result.

_____

_____

_____

_____

(6) Feeding/Off-Bearing.

☐ ☐ ☐
like so-so dislike

Have you ever operated feed machinery, such as a copy machine or printing press?

"Ran copying machine as a student worker in college. Became adept at troubleshooting problems with machine. Result: less lost time due to machine malfunction; reduced costs due to fewer service visits." (Troubleshooting can be important in many jobs. Companies want employees who look ahead and prevent problems because they save the company money.)

What I did; how I did it; why I liked it; the result.

_____

_____

_____

_____

(7) Handling.

☐ ☐ ☐
like so-so dislike

Have you ever sorted and distributed mail or other materials?

"Sorted mail in summer job. Sorted by department and set up a code to speed up process. Result: able to insure mail delivery by 8:30 a.m. every day. Previously, mail was not delivered until 10 a.m. (Efficiency and the ability to organize and expedite work—make it go quickly—are important job skills.)

What I did; how I did it; why I liked it; the result.

_____

_____

_____

_____

Okay, I know you don't want to feed and monitor machines or sort mail. But many of these skills are components of professional jobs. By completing this section you have achieved the following:

- You have identified activities you like to do.

- You have come up with the raw material for your resume and interviewing stories.

The Fun Jobs

Something they never taught you in college is that there are literally thousands of jobs out there that you might like, but they are not necessarily the jobs offered by recruiters who come to campus. For example, suppose you like selling and you love rock music. You might have worked at a retail record shop and combined both of those interests, but you don't want to spend your life selling records at the campus record shop. Most people don't look any further. They forget music and end up selling widgets for an industrial manufacturer. Content to go to concerts on their free time, they never realize that they could spend their careers doing something they really like.

Say you wanted to find a job that combined rock music and selling. Here's an example of a listing in the *Dictionary of Occupational Titles (DOT)* that just might fit the bill.

> **165.157-010 Song Plugger (radio & TV broadcasting)**
> Persuades producers and announcers of radio and television musical shows to broadcast recordings produced by employer: Contacts broadcasting station officials by telephone, letter, or in person. Represents phonograph recording manufacturer in dealing with broadcasters.

Notice the code number next to the song plugger job title: 165.157.010. The "165" part of the code stands for public relations management occupations. The "157" portion refers to the skills needed to do the job. And these are skills you've just finished identifying. According to the *Dictionary*, song plugging requires *Coordinating (1)* from the Information Skills; *Persuading (5)* from the People Skills; and *Handling (7)* from the Materials Skills.

Table of Skills

Data	People	Materials
(0) Synthesizing	(0) Mentoring	(0) Setting up
(1) Coordinating	(1) Negotiating	(1) Precision work
(2) Analyzing	(2) Instructing	(2) Operating/Controlling
(3) Compiling	(3) Supervising	(3) Driving/Operating
(4) Computing	(4) Diverting	(4) Manipulating
(5) Copying	(5) Persuading	(5) Tending
(6) Comparing	(6) Speaking/Signaling	(6) Feeding/Off-Bearing
	(7) Serving	(7) Handling
	(8) Taking instructions Helping	

Look back and note the information, people, and materials skills you really enjoyed. Then comb through the *DOT* at your library to match yourself up with possible jobs.

The *DOT* offers detailed job descriptions that give you a realistic idea of what you will be doing. It gives you an edge over the competition in a job interview because you will be better informed about the requirements of the job and how your skills meet them.

Here's another example from the *DOT* (italics added).

186.117.066 Risk and Insurance Manager
Plans, directs, and coordinates risk and insurance programs of establishment to control risks and losses. *Analyzes and classifies* risks as to frequency and potential severity, and measures financial impact of risk on company. Selects appropriate technique to minimize loss, such as avoidance (reducing chance of loss to zero), loss prevention and reduction (reducing frequency and severity of loss), retention (including self-insurance and planned noninsurance). ... Directs insurance negotiations, selects insurance brokers and carriers, and allocates program costs. Prepares operational and risk reports for management analysis. *Manages* insurance programs, such as fidelity, surety, liability, property, group life, medical, pension plans, and workers' compensation. Prepares operational and risk reports for management analysis. May *negotiate* with unions for employee benefits.

What Is Really Important to You?

"What I really want out of a job is . . ."
   Circle rewards that are very important to you. Ask yourself why they are important. Then put a star next to the top three most important rewards. The job you get should include these three to reduce your risk of personal unhappiness. Jot down the reason why the top three are very important. This exercise takes just a couple of minutes, but it goes a long way toward sorting out priorities.

Money

very important   somewhat important   not important

Why?

_____

_____

_____

Power to make the impact that I feel is important.

very important   somewhat important   not important

Why?

_____

_____

_____

Prestige—I want to be able to impress people.

very important   somewhat important   not important

Why?

_____

_____

_____

Freedom to do the job as I see fit.

    very important   **somewhat important**   **not important**

Why?

_____

_____

_____

Freedom to come and go as I please.

    very important   **somewhat important**   **not important**

Why?

_____

_____

_____

Reward for my efforts.

    very important   **somewhat important**   **not important**

Why?

_____

_____

_____

Security—I don't like risks.

    very important   **somewhat important**   **not important**

Why?

_____

_____

_____

A career track—I'm ambitious and don't want to get stuck in one position too long.

    very important   **somewhat important**   **not important**

Why?

_____

_____

_____

To help people.

    very important   **somewhat important**   **not important**

Why?

_____

_____

_____

Material success—the country club, the Lexus, the Yuppie dream.

    very important   **somewhat important**   **not important**

Why?

_____

_____

_____

To work with friendly people.

    very important   **somewhat important**   **not important**

Why?

_____

_____

_____

To work outdoors.

    very important   **somewhat important**   **not important**

Why?

_____

_____

_____

To use a computer to work on spreadsheets and crunch numbers.

    very important   **somewhat important**   **not important**

Why?

_____

_____

_____

To use a computer for writing.

    very important   **somewhat important**   **not important**

Why?

_____

_____

_____

To meet with the general public every day.

    very important   **somewhat important**   **not important**

Why?

_____

_____

_____

To sell products and earn a commission.

    very important   **somewhat important**   **not important**

Why?

_____

_____

_____

To sell products on straight salary.

    very important   **somewhat important**   **not important**

Why?

_____

_____

_____

To travel.

    very important   **somewhat important**   **not important**

Why?

_____

_____

_____

To each lunch in nice restaurants with clients.

    very important   **somewhat important**   **not important**

Why?

_____

_____

_____

To play golf with clients.

    very important   **somewhat important**   **not important**

Why?

_____

_____

_____

To manage a large staff.

    very important   **somewhat important**   **not important**

Why?

_____

_____

_____

To manage a project.

    very important   **somewhat important**   **not important**

Why?

_____

_____

_____

To work by myself on a project.

    very important   **somewhat important**   **not important**

Why?

_____

_____

_____

To set my own deadlines.

    very important   **somewhat important**   **not important**

Why?

_____

_____

_____

To develop and test new theories.

    very important   **somewhat important**   **not important**

Why?

_____

_____

_____

To work closely with other people on projects.

    very important   **somewhat important**   **not important**

Why?

_____

_____

_____

To supervise people.

    very important   **somewhat important**   **not important**

Why?

_____

_____

_____

To supervise only myself.

very important   somewhat important   not important

Why?

_____

_____

_____

To work only eight hours per day.

very important   somewhat important   not important

Why?

_____

_____

_____

To work 8–12 hours per day if the job requires it.

very important   somewhat important   not important

Why?

_____

_____

_____

To be promoted.

very important   somewhat important   not important

Why?

_____

_____

_____

To work in an expensively decorated, formal office.

    very important   **somewhat important**   **not important**

Why?

_____

_____

_____

To work in a casual, less formal office.

    very important   **somewhat important**   **not important**

Why?

_____

_____

_____

To work for someone who shows me exactly what I should do.

    very important   **somewhat important**   **not important**

Why?

_____

_____

_____

To figure out what to do on my own.

    very important   **somewhat important**   **not important**

Why?

_____

_____

_____

To organize people around an important cause.

   very important   **somewhat important**   **not important**

Why?

_____

_____

_____

To set policy for a large organization.

   very important   **somewhat important**   **not important**

Why?

_____

_____

_____

To have input into policy for a large organization.

   very important   **somewhat important**   **not important**

Why?

_____

_____

_____

To use my creativity.

   very important   **somewhat important**   **not important**

Why?

_____

_____

_____

To have a regular routine every day.

very important　　somewhat important　　not important

Why?

_____

_____

_____

To care for people, take care of them.

very important　　somewhat important　　not important

Why?

_____

_____

_____

To evaluate a situation, determine the cause and fix it.

very important　　somewhat important　　not important

Why?

_____

_____

_____

To have no set routine.

very important　　somewhat important　　not important

Why?

_____

_____

_____

To research, analyze, figure things out.

    very important   **somewhat important**   **not important**

Why?

_____

_____

_____

To evaluate different options and make plans.

    very important   **somewhat important**   **not important**

Why?

_____

_____

_____

To act as second in command.

    very important   **somewhat important**   **not important**

Why?

_____

_____

_____

To own my own business.

    very important   **somewhat important**   **not important**

Why?

_____

_____

_____

To lead or direct other people.

    very important   **somewhat important**   **not important**

Why?

_____

_____

_____

To direct only myself.

    very important   **somewhat important**   **not important**

Why?

_____

_____

_____

To live in a small town.

    very important   **somewhat important**   **not important**

Why?

_____

_____

_____

To live in a big city.

    very important   **somewhat important**   **not important**

Why?

_____

_____

_____

To live near skiing or the ocean, or in warm weather or cold weather.

very important   somewhat important   not important

Why?

_____

_____

_____

To live close to my family.

very important   somewhat important   not important

Why?

_____

_____

_____

To work flexible hours so that I can be with my children.

very important   somewhat important   not important

Why?

_____

_____

_____

To have _____ weeks of vacation per year.

very important   somewhat important   not important

Why?

_____

_____

_____

Go back and look at the rewards you marked very important. These are the qualities about the job that make it important to you. Identify the top three among the very important rewards. Will the job you are considering give you that payoff?

Why should I ask why, you ask? To sort out the true from the inauthentic and find the values that are central to you, at your core. You can take an easy out and say "because it makes me feel good" as an answer to why you want all the things you say you want. But try to go a little deeper. What's underneath? If it's money you want, what does money stand for? Success? More choices? Luxuries? Proving your worth as a person? If the answer has nothing to do with anyone else or anyone else's opinion of you, but is simply deeply in you, then it's natural—part of your basic nature. If it relates to Mom and Dad and what they had or didn't have, is it really relevant to *your* life?

As you evaluate jobs, consider whether they include the rewards you want, then determine whether the market will pay you to do the job. Could you become good enough at the job to command a consultant's fee? If you can, then there is demand for the job and some measure of job security, even if that means working for yourself.

Jobs for which there will never be any reward—internal rewards (fulfillment) or external rewards (money, power, perks, or opportunity to learn a marketable skill)—are not worth your time. Jobs that let you learn a skill and then move on to another skill level, even if they are low-paying, may be worthwhile if the skills you learn are marketable. But it is crucial to determine whether there is a demand for the skills you are learning. If you are in a textile factory learning to sew pants, will you be able to sell that skill to someone else for more money? On the face of it, you may say no. But if you become extremely skilled at a more difficult aspect of the process, and if no one else knows how to do what you do, and if employers need your skills (these are huge "ifs" in the textile industry), then you may be developing a marketable skill. Perhaps you could train other workers in the sophisticated process at another company.

This is your opportunity to find out what you really will be doing on the job and whether it matches your fundamental abilities. Use these sources to identify the primary skills required for various jobs, then match up the requirements to your abilities and interests.

- Use the *Dictionary of Occupational Titles* to find jobs that require your skills.

- Ask your college placement office to show you sample job descriptions from companies that recruit at your school. Compare the skills required with your natural and learned skills.

- Glance over newspaper advertisements to look for jobs requiring your collection of skills.

- Use the information-interviewing procedures outlined in the next chapter to identify potential jobs that require your best skills. Also find out whether any of the jobs you would like to do require an advanced degree.

- Look up careers in another excellent source, the *Occupational Outlook Handbook,* available at most college placement offices and many libraries. The *Handbook* describes the nature of the work, working conditions, job outlook, training needed, salaries, and advancement potential for hundreds of occupations. What's especially good about the *Handbook* is the realistic descriptions of typical work days in a variety of jobs.

Sometimes you can't picture all the possible occupations out there. While the list that follows is by no means complete, it may spark an idea about a job you hadn't thought of before. The list comes from the *Occupational Outlook Handbook.*

Occupations   **Executive, administrative, and managerial occupations**
Bank officers and managers
Health services managers
Hotel managers and assistants
School principals and assistant principals

Management support occupations
Accountants and auditors
Construction and building inspectors
Inspectors and compliance officers, except construction
Personnel, training, and labor relations specialists
Purchasing agents
Underwriters
Wholesale and retail buyers

Engineers, surveyors, and architects
Architects
Surveyors
Aerospace engineers
Chemical engineers
Civil engineers

Electrical and electronics engineers
Industrial engineers
Mechanical engineers
Metallurgical, ceramic, and materials engineers
Mining engineers
Nuclear engineers
Petroleum engineers

Natural scientists and mathematicians
Computer and mathematical occupations
Actuaries
Computer systems analysts
Mathematicians
Statisticians

Physical scientists
Chemists
Geologists and geophysicists
Meteorologists
Physicists and astronomers

Life scientists
Agricultural scientists
Biological scientists/geneticists
Foresters and conservation scientists

Social scientists, social workers, and lawyers
Lawyers
Social scientists and urban planners
Economists
Psychologists
Sociologists
Urban and regional planners

Social and recreation workers
Social workers
Recreation workers

Religious workers
Protestant ministers
Rabbis
Roman Catholic priests

Teachers, counselors, librarians, archivists, and curators
Kindergarten and elementary school teachers
Secondary school teachers
Adult and vocational education teachers

College and university faculty
Counselors
Librarians
Archivists and curators

Health diagnosing and treating practitioners
Chiropractors
Dentists
Optometrists
Physicians
Podiatrists
Veterinarians

Registered nurses, pharmacists, dietitians, therapists, and physician assistants
Dietitians and nutritionists
Occupational therapists
Pharmacists
Physical therapists
Physician assistants
Recreational therapists
Registered nurses
Respirator therapists
Speech pathologists and audiologists

Health technologists and technicians
Clinical laboratory technologists and technicians
Dental hygienists
Dispensing opticians
Electrocardiograph technicians
Electroencephalographic technologists and technicians
Emergency medical technicians
Licensed practical nurses
Medical record technicians
Radiologic technologists
Surgical technicians

Writers, artists, and entertainers; communications occupations
Public relations specialists
Radio and television announcers and newscasters
Reporters and correspondents
Writers and editors

Visual arts occupations
Designers
Graphic and fine artists
Photographers and camera operators

Performing arts occupations
    Actors, directors, and producers
    Dancers and choreographers
    Musicians

Technologists and technicians (except health, engineering, and science technicians)
    Drafters
    Electrical and electronics technicians
    Engineering technicians
    Science technicians

Other technicians
    Air traffic controllers
    Broadcast technicians
    Computer programmers
    Legal assistants
    Library technicians
    Tool programmers, numerical control workers

Marketing and sales occupations
    Cashiers
    Insurance sales workers
    Manufacturers' sales workers
    Real estate agents and brokers
    Retail sales workers
    Securities and financial services sales workers
    Travel agents
    Wholesale trade sales workers

Administrative support occupations, including clerical
    Bank tellers
    Bookkeepers and accounting clerks
    Computer and peripheral equipment operators
    Data entry keyers
    Mail carriers and postal clerks
    Reservation and transportation ticket agents and travel
      clerks
    Secretaries
    Statistical clerks
    Stenographers
    Teacher aides
    Telephone operators
    Traffic, shipping, and receiving clerks
    Typists

Service occupations
    Protective service occupations
    Correction officers

Firefighting occupations
Guards
Police and detectives
Food and beverage preparation and service occupations
Bartenders
Chefs and cooks (except short order)
Waiters and waitresses

Health service occupations
Dental assistants
Medical assistants
Nursing aides and psychiatric aides

Personal service occupations
Barbers
Childcare workers
Cosmetologists and related workers
Flight attendants

Agricultural, forestry, and fishing occupations
Farm operators and managers

Mechanics and repairers
Vehicle and mobile equipment mechanics and repairers
Aircraft mechanics and engine specialists
Automotive and motorcycle mechanics
Automotive body repairers
Diesel mechanics
Farm equipment mechanics
Mobile heavy equipment mechanics

Electrical and electronic equipment repairers
Commercial and industrial electronic equipment
  repairers
Communications equipment mechanics
Computer service technicians
Electronic home entertainment equipment repairers
Home appliance and power tool repairers
Line installers and cable splicers
Telephone installers and repairers
General maintenance mechanics
Heating and air-conditioning mechanics
Refrigeration mechanics
Industrial machinery repairers
Millwrights
Musical instrument repairers and tuners

Office machine and cash register servicers
Vending machine servicers and repairers

Construction and extractive occupations
Bricklayers and stonemasons
Carpenters
Carpet installers
Concrete masons and terrazzo workers
Drywall workers and lathers
Electricians
Glaziers
Insulation workers
Painters and paper hangers
Plasterers
Plumbers and pipefitters
Roofers
Sheet-metal workers
Structural and reinforcing metal workers
Tilesetters

Extractive occupations
Roustabouts

Production occupations
Factory worker supervisor
Precision production occupations
Boilermakers
Bookbinding workers
Butchers and meat-cutters
Compositors and typesetters
Dental laboratory technicians
Jewelers
Lithographic and photoengraving workers
Machinists
Photographic process workers
Shoe and leather workers and repairers
Tool-and-die makers
Upholsterers

Plant and system operators
Stationary engineers
Water and sewage treatment plant operators
Machine operators, tenders, and setup workers
Metalworking and plastic-working machine operators
Numerical-control machine-tool operators
Printing press operators
Fabricators, assemblers, and handworking occupations

Precision assemblers
Transportation equipment painters

Transportation and material moving occupations
Aircraft pilots
Bus drivers
Construction machinery operators
Industrial truck and tractor operators
Truck drivers

Handlers, equipment cleaners, helpers, and laborers
Construction trades helpers

Military occupations

Each of the preceding occupations can be linked to the skills you identified. Some require further education, some don't. *The Dictionary of Occupational Titles* and the *Occupational Outlook Handbook* both provide information on the skills and the everyday duties of the jobs. Look them up. Identify possible jobs and then go to the next chapter for information on how to find out if you will like those jobs.

If You Need More Help in Identifying Your Skills

If working through the skills inventory alone is just not your style—get some help. Go to the counseling and testing center or the university placement center at your college campus and tell them you want help in identifying your skills and interests. Even students who know their career path sometimes need help in narrowing down their field to a job that's right for them. If your university doesn't readily offer these services, talk to the director and to your college dean; this is an essential part of career planning that you have a right to as a student attending a major university. If you attend a small school, talk with faculty members and department heads about available jobs. While most faculty don't see themselves as job placement agents, they should have some knowledge of the real-world problem of translating the educational experience into the marketplace.

If you are not affiliated with a university and you feel you need help in identifying your skills, go to a professional career development agency. Typically these agencies will offer tests administered and interpreted by licensed professional counselors who will spend 4 hours in testing and 4 hours in interpretation and counseling. Costs for the service range from $150 to $800, depending on the market rates for the services in the area. (If you take an hour or so to simply fill in the blanks in this chapter, and you follow the directions for looking up jobs in various books, you can save a lot of money. People I've known who have gone to career counselors rarely felt they got their money's worth. Many counselors will just help you identify your skills. Actually matching them up with jobs and the rest is up to you.) If you do decide to seek out help, Dr. Katherine Boardman of the Career Development Center in Athens, Georgia, offers these tips in evaluating a testing service:

- Be wary of counselors who are reluctant to answer questions about the service.

- A free description of the program should be offered.

- The interpretation should be done by a licensed counselor.

- Be wary of guarantees or sliding payment scales.

- Counselors should have contacts and be able to help you network, but they will not find jobs for you.

- Counselors should help you in finding career areas that are suited to your talents and interests.

Do You Need Another Degree?

Credentials Risk

Now is the time to find out whether you need to go to graduate school to get the job you want.

For the fun of it, let's say you identified four skills from the skills inventory. You liked analysis and instructing, but you also liked persuading and negotiating. Somewhere in the back of your mind, you've thought about a career as a scientific researcher, and you're also attracted to plugging songs for a rock music label. Don't laugh. This is the profile of a person whose mind is wide open, who has a healthy spirit of adventure.

Face-to-Face Research

First, you need to talk to some people who are knowledgeable about both song plugging and scientific research. If you don't know anyone in either field, start by calling a radio station for the names of companies and people who push songs. Next, call the chairman of the science department at a major university. Also, contact the head of the research department of a large company.

Set up appointments with the people you identified to ask questions. This is called information interviewing. You are not looking for a job, just finding out what's going on.

Here's how to do it:

1. Call the person and tell him or her that you are thinking about a career in the field. Emphasize that you are not looking for a job, just information. Make an appointment and assure the person you will not take more than 20 minutes.

2. You may already have questions in mind. If not, consider these questions:

   - What is a typical day like on this job?

   - How is performance evaluated and what is the logical career path?

   - What kind of training and skills are needed to do this job?

   - What advanced degrees are required to do this job?

   - What do you personally like or dislike about this job?

   - What kind of people tend to do well in this job?

   - What is the culture of this industry? Laid back, high-pressure?

   - How did you get into this type of work?

   - At what schools do you recruit new employees? Why do you prefer these schools?

   - During the interview, try to get a sense of what the person you are interviewing is like. What are his or her preferences? Did you have the chance to recommend a book to the person? Following the interview, it would be thoughtful to send him or her a copy of that book. It's not required of course, but it would be a nice gesture.

The information you gather in this 20-minute interview will give you insight not only into the job but also into the atmosphere. Note how people dress and how the office is structured. Ask yourself whether you think you would be happy in this environment. At the end of the interview, thank your source warmly. Send a thank-you note as soon as you get home.

An appropriate thank-you note might say:

Dear Mr. Jones:

Thank you for meeting with me on Monday to discuss career options in the rock music industry. Your insights have given me a more realistic view of what it takes to succeed in this business, and I'm excited about pursuing the next step. I especially enjoyed hearing about your experiences at your first job. I guess things haven't changed very much.

If I can ever be of help to you, I hope you'll give me a call. *(In other words, if there's a way that makes sense to offer to return the favor, offer. For example, if the person is learning to play tennis and expressed an interest in developing his forearm, and you happen to teach tennis, you could offer to give him some lessons.)*

Sincerely,

Joseph Smith

While information interviewing may lead to an offer down the road, some employers see this as a sneaky way to get in for a job interview because this technique has been abused by job seekers. Use these interviews just for information, not as a secret approach to an employer. Be clear that you are not currently seeking a job but are instead seeking information on whether you need another degree or training before entering the field.

How to Find a Good Graduate School

Let's say you realize from the skills inventory and your interviews that you need a graduate degree. Doctoral degrees (Ph.D.s) generally lead to jobs as university professors at research institutions, as teaching professors at colleges or universities, as researchers in industry or the government, and as practitioners, such as psychologists. If you want a Ph.D., you can occasionally enter the program right after you finish your undergraduate degree. The same is true for a J.D. (law degree) or an M.D. (medical degree) though a medical degree will require certain undergraduate course work in the sciences.

Master's degrees can qualify you for a variety of jobs in business and education, often at a slightly higher salary. A few master's degrees, such as the master of social work (M.S.W.), are called terminal degrees and are equivalent to a doctorate. The pay, however, is not equivalent. Check these things out in your interviews with academic departments. They should know starting salaries and placement records of their graduates.

Whether it's for a master's or a doctorate, for a business degree or a degree in the arts and sciences, picking a good graduate school depends on three factors:

1. What is the external reputation of the school? Are the people teaching at the school the recognized leaders in their fields?

2. Do your potential postgraduate employers recruit at the school?

3. How much financial aid can the school put in your pocket?

Notice we're not talking about weather, social life, where your fiancé is, etc. You will need to move from graduate school into the kind of job you really want. Don't go to an inferior school; you will always regret it.

Be selective about the institution you choose. The quality of graduate programs differs widely. You don't want to invest 2 to 4 years in an advanced degree program only to find out that the reputation of your school will get you offers only from inferior schools or companies. Just because a certain school has a good reputation overall doesn't mean the department you are looking at has a good reputation. Recruiting literature may claim prestigious placements and fail to mention that the placements were made 10 years ago. Get current placement and salary information.

To find out if the school is good, ask your current college professors to identify the top school in the field. If you want an engineering degree and you're working on a math degree, go to the engineering department of your present institution, rather than the math department, and ask the professors the names of the best schools.

To find out the placement record, ask the companies you want to work for when you get out where they recruit students. Don't sign up with a school until you have talked with at least three potential employers about where they recruit. They are your market. Ask the college where last year's graduates were placed. If they don't know or give you a hazy answer, they still may be placing students, but it's obviously not a top priority for them.

If you want a job as an industrial researcher, ask the top people in the research and development departments of major industries if they recruit the graduates of the schools you are considering. If no one recruits at your school, a degree from that school won't help you. The same is true for graduate programs preparing you for a career in academics. Call the department heads at schools where you would eventually like to work and ask where they recruit their new Ph.D.s or M.B.A.s. They will probably be happy to talk with you about the quality of various programs.

The M.B.A. Alternative

What about getting an M.B.A.? Increasingly, M.B.A.s are required for upper-level management. The most potent combination of credentials in the business job market is an M.B.A. plus a few years of work experience. Although some students like to go straight through from an undergraduate to graduate school, they have a harder time finding a job without work experience. Though M.B.A.s are required for many jobs, and search firms say you are more marketable with one, inexperienced M.B.A.s have flooded the market recently. If you decide to go straight through, get a summer job as an intern so that you have some work experience on your resume as well as a few contacts.

If you have a good grade point average or you tend to score high on standardized tests, shoot for the best M.B.A. program you can get into, preferably at a school other than your undergraduate school. When you go to a new school, you are exposed to different ideas and instructors. If you remain at your undergraduate school, you may have the same courses with only the numbers changed. The best programs often require you to work for a year or two before applying, though some will let you in without work experience. Check out the annual *BusinessWeek* survey for an up-to-date listing of good programs at state and private institutions.

If you can't afford an M.B.A. right now, look into companies that will pay for your education. Or work for a couple of years and save your money. Get student loans and invest your money in yourself.

If your standardized test scores tend to be low, or your grade point average is under a B average, check into graduate programs that have less stringent requirements but have good placement records. Do this by calling major companies in the part of the country where the school is located. Ask where they recruit their M.B.A.s. This tells you how the market evaluates the school. In general, don't listen to what the school says about itself; listen to the market. The recruiters may prefer a certain school because they have had good luck with the referrals from that school. It may be a private or a state school. You can check with the school's placement office, though placement offices rarely have reliable information that can be easily compared with data from other placement offices. The marketplace is your best source.

For lists of top-rated M.B.A. programs, check out lists published in *U.S. News and World Report* and the survey published in *BusinessWeek*.

The Doctoral Alternative

If you want an academic job, a good way to look at advanced degree programs is by reading the top academic journals in your field to determine who the top researchers are. You can do this by first finding out which are the top journals in your area. Ask a professor which journals researchers must publish in to get tenure. Then comb through several recent issues to see the names most often cited at the ends of the articles. Next, find out where those persons work. Go where the top people are if you can. You will learn more and you will have the opportunity of having a leading researcher back you when you go into the job market. Proteges often get jobs more easily because departments in lesser-known schools want to curry the favor of famous researchers.

If you seek a job as a professor at a research university, the Ph.D. program should be good enough to get you offers from comparable research schools. When checking out potential schools, always get a list of schools or companies that have hired their graduates during the last four years. Doctoral programs should have such a list on hand. If they don't know where their graduates have placed, you don't want anything to do with them.

Non-research teaching positions are less prestigious and pay less than research jobs, but they still require doctorates from good institutions. Colleges hiring professors for teaching positions can be fussy about the pedigrees of their hires. Often even junior colleges require a Ph.D. these days; therefore, if you want to teach on the college level, you will need an advanced degree from a school that is respected by your potential job market.

Most graduate schools require solid standardized test scores, a high GPA, and recommendations from academic sources (professors). The top tier of schools—Harvard, Stanford, Cal Tech, MIT, Cornell, Brown, the University of Chicago, and others—is expensive, but financial aid is available.

A good standardized test score on the Graduate Management Admissions Test (GMAT) or Graduate Record Examination (GRE) puts you in the 90th percentile or above. Top schools can recruit students with nearly perfect scores, while second- and third-tier schools will recruit from the 90+ and 80+ pool. Many schools will often accept students with low standardized test scores if they have high GPAs and good recommendations from recognized undergraduate programs.

Take both the GMAT and the GRE if you are applying to a business graduate program. (The LSAT is required for law school.) The graduate school at your current institution can advise you on test dates and requirements. Prepare for the test by taking a test preparation course. If you take it and don't do well, take it again. Retaking the tests can boost scores by as much as 30 points. Since admissions screens may eliminate you if your score is too low, go ahead and boost your score as much as possible.

What if your scores are on the low side and your GPA is nothing to brag about? It may be a long shot, but if you have skills to offer (research, computer skills, the ability to do grunt work willingly), you might try to get admitted as a transient student or student-at-large and offer to do the grunt work for a top researcher in your area. Introduce yourself to the researcher and be enthusiastic about the work. After you have proven yourself, the researcher may help you get full admission.

Publishing paves the way to success in academics. If you can work with your famous researcher and get your name on a paper and get it published, you have begun to write your own ticket in academics. You have what academics live for, a publication and a recommendation from a top researcher. Now go back and apply to the schools you are interested in; you may find that the doors previously closed to you will be thrown open. Be aware, though, that this process might take 2 to 5 years. The wheels of academic publishing turn slowly.

Publishing will pave the way for both admission and financial aid in doctoral programs. Since money to pay for graduate assistantships and fellowships is scarce, and academic departments often must compete against each other for graduate study stipends, you have a better chance of receiving aid if you have published. Publications may give you an edge over other students with good grades and with high GPAs but no publications. If you look better on paper to the graduate committee than the contenders from other departments for financial awards, your department won't have to dip into its own funds to pay your stipend. Annual stipends paid to graduate assistants in Ph.D. programs can range from $8,000 to $17,000 per year. In some cases out-of-state tuition is waived as well.

Financing Graduate School

Using a combination of grants, scholarships, and student loans, you can finance your tuition and living expenses, but be careful about the level of debt you take on. The cost of getting an M.B.A. can range from only $9,500 at the University of Georgia to more than $30,000 at Northwestern University as of this writing. The Georgia program can be completed in either one or two years. Obviously, one year in school is cheaper than two. The costs involved in getting a Ph.D. or J.D. can be higher because the programs take longer.

Think of your financial aid package as an investment. What will the return be on your investment? If you invest $10,000 from a guaranteed student loan, will the job you get when you get out allow you to repay your debt comfortably?

A recent story in *The Wall Street Journal* by Joan Rigdon about financial aid should serve as a warning. One student with a graduate degree in social work had borrowed $25,000 to finance her master's degree from the University of California at Berkeley. When she went into the job market, she was shocked to qualify only for jobs paying in the $18,000 to $25,000 per year range. Her student loan payments of $350 per month restrict her lifestyle severely. She lives with her parents.

Rigdon reported that another student borrowed $15,000 to receive an undergraduate degree in English. His "hoped for" job as an entry-level employee at a publishing house would have paid him only $6.00 per hour, a salary that would have not allowed him to both make his $150 per month debt payments and pay the rent. As a result, he took a job as a welder—it's not his chosen field, but it pays the bills.

Tips for Calculating How Much to Borrow

1. Find out how much you can expect to earn when you get out of school by asking the graduate coordinator of the programs you are considering about typical entry-level salaries in various parts of the country. Don't trust the school's word alone. Contact the companies that recruit at your school and ask for information on typical starting salaries.

2. Estimate the size of a car payment if you were to buy a new or used car when you graduate. As of this writing, a new economical four-door car, such as a Ford Taurus or Mazda, will cost you $250 to $275 per month for the next five years. In addition, the purchase will require 10 percent down, about $1,400.

3. Consider whether or not you will be comfortable sharing rent with a roommate or whether you need your own place. Calculate the cost of rent in various parts of the country. One way to do this is to go to a large library and read the housing ads to compare apartment rents.

4. Ask the financial aid office for a debt repayment schedule to calculate the size of your monthly payments based on the amount you borrow.

5. Borrow only the absolute minimum you need to get into the best program with the highest long-term return.

Financial aid programs require you to meet application deadlines like no other business. The bureaucracy takes several months to process your guaranteed student loan. If you apply early enough, you may even qualify for grants, scholarships, and assistantships. If possible, apply by January for September admission.

The amount of stipends awarded at various institutions varies widely. Some schools have large endowments. The income from endowments supplements the operating income these schools receive from tuition and tax dollars. Some individual departments have their own endowments as well. Thus, the first place to ask about financial aid is at the academic department you are applying to. The graduate coordinator of the department you are considering should be able to provide you with an estimate of your potential financial aid package.

Armed with the departmental information, send for the student financial aid package and complete all the forms necessary to qualify for aid. If you are early enough, you may get a chance at applying for a grant or scholarship. If you are not eligible for one of these, you may want to take out a student loan.

Of course, your primary goal is to receive free money that you don't have to pay back, in the form of fellowships or scholarships. The earlier you apply, the better your chances. That means applying for admission to as many colleges as you wish to attend during or before January if you plan to attend the following September. The only way that you will be able to compare aid packages is by actually applying and being accepted at more than one institution. The financial aid offices will not take the time to speculate on how much money you could make if you were admitted. They will help only if you actually are admitted. That way you don't lose out on possible funding and you can compare the funding packages at various institutions.

The Guaranteed Student Loan Program will advance you up to $7,500 per year at 8 percent interest (as of 1/91). To qualify, you must meet strict financial need guidelines. You can qualify as an independent (that means they will look only at your financial data and not your parents) if you are one of the following: older than 24, a ward of the court, a veteran, or if you have a dependent other than a spouse. If you don't fall into any of these categories, you are considered a dependent, and your aid determination will depend on how much money, assets, and expenses your parents have. Your need is based on how much you need to attend school when your family's contribution is subtracted.

The Guaranteed Student Loan Program works this way:

- First, you apply and become admitted to an approved college program.

- Next, you fill out the application supplied by the student financial aid office and send the completed application to one of four service centers for processing. (They will tell you where.) The service centers examine your assets, income, and other financial data to determine the level of your need.

- If you qualify, then the financial aid office determines your eligibility and sends you out to look for a lender, usually a local bank. Banks may impose additional requirements to reduce risk. For example, a local bank in Georgia requires recipients of student loans to have had a checking account with the institution for one year prior to the loan and a grade point average of 2.0 or better. These requirements are intended to reduce the risk.

- Very important: Keep all your students loans at one bank. If you have multiple loans at different banks the banks may not consolidate your loan. And since these loans carry a minimum of $50 per month payment, you could end up paying $200 per month on loans at four banks, but would have paid only $50 per month on the same amount at one bank.

- You will have to pay an origination fee for the loan equal to 5 percent of the amount you borrow.

- Interest rates on these loans are much lower than market rates on consumer loans.

Repayment of the loan will start six months after you graduate. The six-month grace period helps you get on your feet, buy a car, put down a deposit on an apartment, and get a job.

Incidentally, the government is considering revising the Guaranteed Student Loan Program to eliminate the banks, in order to simplify the paperwork and reduce the time it takes to get you your money. But as of this writing, it still takes several months to get the loan processed. To avoid getting stuck with an extra bank loan to tide you over until your student loan comes through, apply early. And remember, the earlier you apply, the better your chances of getting free money that you don't have to pay back.

Reducing Rubber Check Risk

Getting a Job Right Away

What about getting a job right away? That's what my graduate advisor told me to do when I asked him if I could get a graduate assistantship some 20 years ago. "What!" I said. I was appalled at the idea of going out and getting a job. After all, I majored in art history, a ladylike career with virtually no future except for graduate school or sales in an art gallery, and I had had my fill of art school. I wanted a graduate degree in public relations because although I didn't feel qualified to do anything, I knew I could write. My professor just pulled a piece of paper out of a drawer in his desk and told me to call this person about a job. It was a fund-raising job for a small college.

I needed the money, and figured, What the heck? I called, got the job, and spent three years raising money for Ronald Reagan's alma mater. I learned more on the job than I ever would have in graduate school.

You may wonder why Ronald Reagan's alma mater hired an art history major with no experience. The only answer I can offer is that I was a political organizer in college for the McGovern campaign. My limited political experience helped me more than any college course, except for the excellent training I received in the one public relations course I had—the course taught by the instructor who pushed me out the door into the world of work. He gave me a good recommendation.

So, how did I get my first job? Through a contact who gave me a good recommendation. Not from a want ad, not from a search firm, not from a campus recruiter. One of the best ways by far to get a job is through a contact, even a contact who is a stranger.

Fifty People Who Can Help You Get a Job Right Away

Let's say you are interested in the song plugging career discussed in earlier chapters. Your calls to local radio stations got you names of companies and people who do that type of work. You may have had information interviews with them already, but you still need to find out more and create more contacts. Maybe you want to plug songs in Denver, or maybe you haven't yet identified people who can help you.

Discipline yourself to sit down and make a list of fifty people you know. They don't have to be close friends or friends at all. These people may be the key to helping you get into the job market, just as my public relations professor helped me. You can write down the names of teachers, your little brother's baseball coach, your mother's bridge group, members of your church or temple, other students, friends of your father, uncles and aunts, neighbors.

Use every inside contact you have. This is not the time to be proud, or to say, "I've got to do it all on my own." All your inside contact will do is help you get your foot in the door to get an interview. After that, you are on your own.

If you taught tennis to executives who told you to look them up when you got out of school, by all means, look them up. If your girlfriend's uncle said he would get you an interview, let him do it. On the outside, you are one of thousands of fish in the sea. On the inside, you have a chance.

You will find that most people are happy to help you out. After all, they are just giving you a name of someone who works at a company. You'd be amazed at how people like to help people, even people they don't know. It's not as if they will be recommending you for a job; they are just giving you a name—an inside contact whom you can call. You need inside contacts to help you get interviews. Start with your parents; then fill in friends, relatives, alumni, professors, former teachers, church members and politicians. Ask each of these groups for contacts.

Your Fifty-Plus Contacts

Dad's, uncle's, brother's, college professor's, friends of friends' contacts.
People he knows who work in similar jobs at his company or other companies.

	Name	Phone
1.		
2.		
3.		
4.		
5.		

People he knows who live in the town where you want to go.

	Name	Phone
1.		
2.		
3.		
4.		
5.		

People he knows who go to your church or synagogue.

	Name	Phone
1.		
2.		
3.		
4.		
5.		

People he golfs with, plays tennis with, plays racquetball with.

Name   Phone

1. _____

2. _____

3. _____

4. _____

5. _____

People he is distantly or closely related to.

Name   Phone

1. _____

2. _____

3. _____

4. _____

5. _____

People he knows from the parents group at your high school (band, baseball volunteers, prom chaperones).

Name   Phone

1. _____

2. _____

3. _____

4. _____

5. _____

People he knows from professional organizations.

Name   Phone

1. _____

2. _____

3. _____

4. _____

5. _____

Neighbors.

Name   Phone

1. _____

2. _____

3. _____

4. _____

5. _____

Mom's, professor's, stepmother's, sister's, aunt's, former supervisor's contacts:
People she knows who work in a similar job at her company.

Name   Phone

1. _____

2. _____

3. _____

4. _____

5. _____

People she knows who live in the town where you want to go.

Name   Phone

1. _____

2. _____

3. _____

4. _____

5. _____

People she knows who go to your church or synagogue.

Name   Phone

1. _____

2. _____

3. _____

4. _____

5. _____

People she knows from her bridge or golf club.

Name   Phone

1. _____

2. _____

3. _____

4. _____

5. _____

People she is distantly or closely related to.

Name   Phone

1. _____

2. _____

3. _____

4. _____

5. _____

People she knows from the parents group at your high school (band, baseball volunteers, prom chaperones).

Name   Phone

1. _____

2. _____

3. _____

4. _____

5. _____

People she knows from professional organizations.

Name   Phone

1. _____

2. _____

3. _____

4. _____

5. _____

Neighbors she knows.

Name   Phone

1. _____

2. _____

3. _____

4. _____

5. _____

Your former employer's contacts (part-time or college jobs).

Name   Phone

1. _____

2. _____

3. _____

4. _____

5. _____

High school teacher's contacts.

Name   Phone

1. _____

2. _____

3. _____

4. _____

5. _____

Minister's or priest's contacts.

    Name   Phone

1. _____

2. _____

3. _____

4. _____

5. _____

Congressman's contacts.

    Name   Phone

1. _____

2. _____

3. _____

4. _____

5. _____

Alderman's or elected ward official's contacts.

    Name   Phone

1. _____

2. _____

3. _____

4. _____

5. _____

Roommate's contacts.

	Name	Phone
1.	_____	
2.	_____	
3.	_____	
4.	_____	
5.	_____	

Call each of these people and tell them you are in the job market and interested in a specific industry, city, company, type of job. Don't be shy, just be courteous and likeable.

How to Approach Your Contacts

If you are looking for information about a specific industry (e.g., song plugging, newspapers, computers, medicine, social service agencies, banks, etc.):

Call everyone on the list and tell them you are in the job market, and that you are trying to find out general information on the job outlook in your industry. You are not asking them for a job, you are merely asking if they know anyone in the industry who might be able to provide you with general information. Keep in mind that the names they give you will probably be *their* friends or neighbors. Maybe your uncle plays racquetball with someone who works in the industry. When you call your uncle's contact, you may find he does not work in the department you are interested in, but he may suggest that you talk with someone else. This is the beginning of the chain.

If you are looking for information about a specific company:

Ask about contacts they may have at specific companies. Ask them if they would share the names and phone numbers.

If you are looking for information about a different part of the country:

If you want to work in Denver, and you live in Des Moines, ask everyone on your list first if he or she knows anyone who lives in Denver.

This process of being passed along from one person to another is called networking. You are not asking for a job, just information—about a company, about a city, about a typical day in a career.

When you get someone on the phone, tell him or her who referred you and what you want. For example:

"This is John Brown. Bill Edwards suggested I call you because I'm trying to find out information about job opportunities in the field of risk management. I wondered if you might have a few minutes to talk with me about the outlook at XYZ Industries, either on the phone or in person."

Don't expect him or her to talk with you on the spot. Ask if there is a convenient time to call back or come in.

The person may not be in the risk management department, but may know someone else who is. You might chat for a few minutes about your mutual contact. And then the person may give you a name of someone you could call in the risk management department.

Or you might call someone's aunt's cousin who lives in Denver, explain who you are and that you will be looking for work in the Denver area. Ask what the economy is like there. Tell him or her what industry you are interested in and then ask if he or she knows anyone in the industry. Then get on the phone again.

Eventually, you will talk with someone in the right department and the right industry and the right city. Again, use your mutual contact's name right away in the phone conversation. Then ask about the job outlook in the field he or she is in. Ask if you could set up a time to discuss the field to get an idea if you would like that kind of work. Or, be more direct and tell the person you are looking for a position in that department and that you would like to send a resume. Be sure to have a concise, catchy way to describe what you've done. Look over your skills inventory for an example.

What if you can't find anyone who knows anything about your chosen areas? Walk your resume directly to the person who can hire you (not the personnel office). If it's a very small company, make an appointment to see the president or an executive vice president if you are seeking a professional job. One client I work with owns a small business. He says that the best way to get an interview is to dress well, walk into the company, and ask to see the president. He expects job applicants to have researched his company and to be enthusiastic about wanting to work for his company.

Telephone Each of the Companies You Are Interested In

1. Find out how they *say* they want to be approached. You can find out a lot from people who work in the personnel department if you are polite and don't take up too much of their time. (If it's a big company, you

might not get through at all. In that case, find an inside contact.)

2. Ask when the recruiter is coming to your campus
   and how you can get your name on the interviewing
   list. If the company doesn't come to your campus, ask
   how you can set up an interview.

3. Find out which jobs they are recruiting for. Ask for
   job descriptions.

4. Request company information on careers in different
   areas: production management, accounting, finance,
   information technology, etc.

The 90s Approach: Internships and Contract Work

While you are still in school or even after you have graduated, you can get inside by contacting companies and arranging to work on internships. Get internships with as
many firms as possible. Try out two or three fields while
you are still in school or even during the year following
graduation. You will get a realistic idea of what the job is
like and make valuable contacts. These are often your best
job leads, and they give you exposure to the work environment. Check with your college advisor to determine
whether you can do an internship for academic credit.

It has become fairly common for employers to hire professionals on a contractual basis before giving them a full-
time job. Architects, accountants, and other professionals
with skills to offer are being asked to work part-time or on
a project-by-project basis to prove their worth to cash-short
firms. This gives you a chance to check out a company, and
vice versa. But before signing, find out what percentage of
their contract workers eventually get offered full-time jobs.
You need medical insurance and other benefits contract
workers don't get. Explore this option only if it is short-
term or if you have someone who can carry you on his or
her health insurance policy (working spouse or parents).

Government internships can offer good experience and the
chance to work full-time for the government later on. You
can apply directly to federal agencies anywhere in the country for an internship or co-op position (a job where you work
on an alternating semester basis—one semester you work,
the next, you're in school), and often the government will provide a co-op position that also gives you academic credit.
These positions are becoming more available lately since hir-

ing freezes (especially in the defense industry) have pre-
vented government agencies from hiring permanent workers.

If you have high grades, ask the dean of your college to
recommend you for the Presidential Management Internship
Program, a two-year training program that results in entry
into upper-level management and pay at the GS9 level
($27,000 in 1992). After two years, you can earn as much as
$40,000. The federal government reserves 400 spots for Presi-
dential Management Interns, and only 850 apply each year.
Some states have never even nominated a student for the
program. If you reside in a state where this has not been promoted, such as South Carolina, you have a good chance of being accepted, according to a federal personnel specialist who
provided information on this program. The selection process
can take up to a year. For more information on the Presidential Management Internship, call 912/757-3000.

Be Visible   You need visibility and you need to show people what you
are capable of doing. Join associations or clubs that are of
genuine interest to you, take on a project, and develop a
reputation.

Professional associations are generally useful. Toast-
masters, a public speaking club, can sometimes be good,
depending on the local membership. Rotary and other fra-
ternal organizations can be useful as well. The people you
meet there can go on your list of fifty people to ask about
jobs, companies, and cities.

The following professional associations offer information about membership in their organizations. Call them
for general information on your field and advice.

Professional Associations

Associations	City/State	Telephone
American Association of Engineering Societies	Washington, DC	202/296-2237
American Association of Museums	Washington, DC	202/289-1818
American Chemical Society	Washington, DC	202/872-4600
American Home Economics Association	Alexandria, VA	703/706-4600
American Public Power Association	Washington, DC	202/467-2900
American Society of Association Executives	Washington, DC	202/626-2723
American Society of Information Science	Silver Spring, MD	301/495-0900
American Society of Landscape Architects	Washington, DC	202/686-2752

Associations	City/State	Telephone
American Society for Quality Control	Milwaukee, WI	414/272-8575
American Society of Safety Engineers	Des Plaines, IL	708/692-4121
Club Managers Association of America	Alexandria, VA	703/739-9500
College Placement Council	Bethlehem, PA	215/868-1421
Geological Society of America	Boulder, CO	303/447-2020
Greater Washington Society of Association Executives	Washington, DC	202/429-9370
Public Relations Society of America	New York, NY	212/995-2230
Printing Industries of America	Arlington, VA	703/841-8100
Society for Human Resource Management	Alexandria, VA	703/548-3440
Society of Professional Journalists	Greencastle, IN	317/653-3333
Society of Research Administrators	Chicago, IL	312/661-1700
Women in Communications Inc.	Arlington, VA	703/528-4200

Do You Need a Search Firm?

Search firms generally will not take on entry-level employees because employers won't pay a fee for new recruits. If you are an experienced worker, be wary of search firms. Their placement counselors are usually paid on a commission basis, and no matter how much they profess to be looking out for everyone's interests, they really only care about the interests of the person footing the bill—and that is the employer. Go ahead and interview with companies the search firm finds, but check out the companies yourself. Don't rely too heavily on what the recruiter says about the company. The recruiter is trying to make a sale.

Interview with as many companies as possible to increase the chances of getting an offer. Don't interview with companies you know you don't want to work for. There's no point in wasting their time and yours.

Campus interviewers sometimes pre-screen the list of applicants, eliminating students with grade-point averages below 3.0. If you find out that your company does this screening, and your GPA is below 3.0, contact the company yourself with a letter and phone call explaining that you would like to interview anyway.

Phone Tag and Other Games

If you have built up good will by using an inside contact to smooth the way, you will have an easier time on the phone when you call to set up the appointment. If you are lucky enough to get the person on the line whom you sent the letter to, you can say:

"This is June Luckhart. I sent you a letter last week requesting an interview for the management training program. John Doe suggested I contact you."

What if you get the secretary instead? A big mistake many job seekers make is treating the secretary like furniture or an obstacle to be overcome. Instead, recognize that the boss's secretary may carry much more power than you realize. Often a boss will come out of the outer office after an interview and ask the secretary's opinion on the applicant. If the applicant whizzed past the secretary as if he or she was unimportant, it will be noticed. On the telephone, write down the secretary's name as soon as he or she gives it to you. Identify yourself and explain why are are calling. There's no point in being sneaky and trying to pretend you are calling about some other business. Be sure to name your contact, though. If your contact is someone inside the company, the secretary might take your request more seriously and put you through to the boss. Or the secretary may schedule your interview herself. Be sure to have your calendar and a pen ready, just in case.

What if the boss is not there and the secretary doesn't want to help? Be friendly, ask when would be a convenient time to reach the boss. You can get an idea about what kind of organization it is by how available the boss is to the public. While presidents and CEOs should have the secretary screen calls, lower-level officials who are inaccessible to calls from people like you probably work in a highly structured, noncompetitive business. When business is competitive, there are fewer employees sitting around screening calls. When a business is driven by customer service, managers don't shy away from the public. Tax-supported organizations, however, haven't caught on that they have customers.

People who are on top of things often answer their own phones. People who work in rigid bureaucracies, such as universities, federally supported agencies, or hospitals, sometimes use multiple screens to protect themselves from phone calls. They pay secretaries to keep the world at a safe distance.

If a boss is never available to the public, how will the boss find out what's wrong with the product or service? How will the boss know about employee's feelings? In this day and age, exactly why is this person a boss if he or she is not accessible? You can't manage a program by hiding behind a desk and never leaving your office. Management means you are with and around people—a lot.

There may be some people who don't answer their phones who turn out to be great bosses. But the more screens they set up to keep you out, the more rigid the organization. If there are still layers of screens to keep the public at bay in the 1990s, then the company has not yet undergone the downsizing that most companies will face in this decade. Companies competing in the marketplace don't have enough cash to protect small-fry managers. In fact, good companies want their managers in touch, not protected.

What if you do get through and you actually have a live potential boss on the other end of the line? First, smile. Even though the boss can't see you, you will sound and feel friendlier if you smile when you are speaking. Identify yourself and the contact you have. Don't ask if the boss has reviewed your resume; assume he or she has. Ask if there would be a convenient time to get together to talk. The boss may refer you to the secretary for an appointment. Or the boss may say that he or she hasn't had a chance to look at the resume yet. If so, ask when would be a good time to call back. Make all your conversation upbeat, positive. Don't apologize for calling or for anything else. You are the winner, the one they want to hire and no one else. Don't forget it. There simply is no competition.

Resume and Cover Letter Risk 5

Don't Get Stuck on the Bottom of the Pile

According to corporate staffing manager Keith Johnson, recruiters ask themselves three questions about every job applicant:

> *Can* the applicant do the job?
> *Will* the applicant do the job?
> Will the applicant *fit in*?

A good resume should answer two of those questions. It should show that you *can* do the job—it should show your intelligence, grades, work experience, and the quality of your schooling. The resume should also show the potential employer that you *will* do the job, that you are responsible, can achieve goals, show up for work, and can be trusted to follow through. Your record of achievement in part-time work, clubs, and academics provides important information on your willingness to work. The resume should catch the employer's interest so that they will want to meet you in an interview to determine the answer to the last question: Will you fit in?

In preparing a resume, use evidence and objective praise to demonstrate your strong points. *Never, never lie.* Besides being unethical and creating bad karma, lies make you uneasy; and recruiters will have a sixth sense about your unease.

Think of a resume as a news story. The headline is the job objective; the details supporting the headline are your education, activities, and work experience. Sometimes you need to look below the surface of jobs you've had to uncover the skill that you developed in that job. For example, say you were applying for an entry-level position as a programmer/analyst. You would certainly want to play up your experience in computer classes or computer clubs. If you produced a program or know several computer languages, emphasize this knowledge. If you have substantial work experience, play up the experience that most directly relates to the job you are applying for.

Here's a fairly typical student who is stumped about how to prepare his resume. He would really like to start his own business, and he wants help.

Student: "Well, I really haven't done much of anything to put on a resume. I had a job at McDonald's in high school, and I made pizzas in college. I really don't have any experience, and I don't know why anyone would take a chance on me."

Advisor: "So, somehow you've gotten to be a senior in college with a reasonably decent grade point average, you've held down a part-time job, and you have no skills?"

Student: "Well, the stuff I've done isn't the kind of thing I see on resumes. Everyone always has all these clubs that they're president of, and they always have super-high GPAs. . . ."

Advisor: "Those achievements are fine, but they really don't tell recruiters as much as you think. If students have sky-high grades, but they never do anything outside of going to class, the recruiter might wonder about their social skills. Did the club president really accomplish anything? Good recruiters look deeper than the surface. Your achievements may be different and may actually relate to the job more."

Student: "What do you mean?"

> *Advisor:* "Have you ever had a job that you started yourself, like a lawn-trimming service in high school? Or have you ever received any recognition for the work you did at the pizza place or McDonald's?"
>
> *Student:* "Well, I didn't have a lawn service, but I did start selling gold jewelry on the side in college. I made $4,000 in two years. And I did get quite a compliment from the boss at the pizza job because I sold more pizza packages to fraternities for parties than anyone else."
>
> *Advisor:* "These are significant achievements. They show sales skill, initiative, and entrepreneurial drive."

This is the thinking process that begins to relate what you have done to what you want to do. To convert these skills into work experience or achievements on a resume, use action verbs.

For example:

19---present   **Counter Clerk**
Pizza Now/Bloomfield, Maine
Responsible for selling party packages.
- Sold 800 party packages during homecoming, which surpassed the store record by 200 packages.
- Promoted to outside salesperson after one year.

19---present   **Owner**
Gold and Gems Jewelry
Set up personal gold jewelry sales business out of dorm room.
- Earned $4,000 in two years by displaying and selling jewelry, purchased from local wholesaler.

General Resume Hints

We will go through resume preparation step by step. Keep this general approach in mind and come back and review these tips to be sure your finished product covers these points.

- Include your most significant achievements in the upper two-thirds of the resume. Most recruiters spend 20 seconds or less reviewing your resume.

- Use only one page unless you have significant work experience.

- Use no more than three forms of formatting (upper- and lower-case headings, boldface)

- Make it easy to read. Do not use a photograph unless you are applying for a theatrical or modeling position. Personnel managers can be sticky about this for fear of lawsuits or discrimination cases.

- Use heavy white, gray, or ecru bond paper (60 or 70 lb.).

- Use action verbs and phrases rather than complete sentences.

- Type up your resume on a computer that prints in laser type. Save your disc and update your resume as needed. Take the laser master to a copy center to have copies made on good paper. Don't have copies made from copies, only from the laser master; otherwise, the copies may not be as sharp.

- Don't include personal information: health, age, marital state, or race.

How Should I Organize My Resume?

Most employers prefer that you list your education and jobs from the most recent to the most distant, in reverse chronological order. If your most recent job is not clearly related to the job you are seeking, you may want to emphasize the previous job instead. In that case, you would list the most relevant job first. Be aware, however, that this non-typical format may raise questions in a potential employer's mind.

The Energy Center Theory

The energy center is where you put most of your energy, and everyone has one. Your energy center may be in student activities and clubs. It may be in working several jobs and putting yourself through school. It may be in academics, in achieving all A's. It may be in sports, intramural or collegiate. It may be in getting along with people, or listening to their problems, or doing handwork, or buying cars and fixing them up, or sculpting, or tutoring kids, or doing precise laboratory work, or computer programming, or playing the trumpet. Wherever the energy center is, there is achievement. And wherever there is achievement, there are skills that have been developed.

The challenge is to identify the energy center on your resume and balance it. For example, if most of your achievement is in club work, balance that by listing significant course work. If most of your energy is in academics, look for activity and work examples to present a well-rounded picture.

Resume Structure

You can take some liberties with structure. Your name, of course, must be at the top with your address and phone; after that, use the structure that puts your best foot forward. Put your strongest selling point at the top. Selling points can be grades, activities, work experience, or even volunteer work. There are no hard and fast rules.

Name and Address

Put your name, centered, at the top of the resume. Use a larger point size for your name. List your campus and your home address. Here are three types of headings.

Example 1: centered name, two addresses

JOSEPH SMITH

Current Address:	**Permanent Address:**
222 Campus Street	189 Golf Course Drive
Campus City, Georgia 54444	Ritzy-Ritz, Georgia 55555
(404) 555-5555	(404) 555-5555

Example 2: left justified with double line

JOSEPH SMITH
═══════════════════════════════════════

Current Address:	**Permanent Address:**
222 Campus Street	189 Golf Course Drive
Campus City, Georgia 54444	Ritzy-Ritz, Georgia 55555
(404) 555-5555	(404) 555-5555

Example 3: one address

JOSEPH SMITH

189 Golf Course Drive

Ritzy-Ritz, Georgia 55555

(404) 555-5555

Job Objective   You will change it often. Don't feel married to one objective. The more you learn about yourself and your market, the more often you will update your job objective.

Use your skills and research in the *Dictionary of Occupational Titles* to pinpoint either a specific job (for example, an entry-level position in a commercial bank management training program) or a job related to the skills you want to use on the job, such as, "an entry-level position that requires analytical ability, understanding of computer modeling, and writing skills." Or simply use the title of the job you are applying for. Customize the resume for every job: "A position with Kraft Foods as a Market Analyst."

Tip: Get a copy of the job description for the job you are applying for and rephrase it.

Here are some examples of objectives:

OBJECTIVE: An entry-level position in insurance underwriting.

OBJECTIVE: A position that requires knowledge of decision-making models and computer programming.

OBJECTIVE: An entry-level position that requires strong writing and television production skills and experience in dealing with the media.

OBJECTIVE: Commercial bank management training.

OBJECTIVE: General Sales Representative for the chemical industry.

OBJECTIVE: Account Representative with ABC Industrials.

OBJECTIVE: Field Services Administrator for DATA International.

OBJECTIVE: Training Coordinator for Elrod Industries.

OBJECTIVE: Art Instructor/Elementary Education.

Do You Really Need a Job Objective?   Sometimes yes, sometimes no.

The following ideas apply to entry-level workers and new college grads. Experienced workers *usually* should have an objective, but not always.

You may not need to list a job objective if:

1. You are going to grad school and are sending your resume to a school.

2. If you have set up interviews with high-level officers of a company that has several different openings and you don't want to limit yourself to one area.

3. If you really don't know what you want to do.

4. If you are not comfortable with a job objective.

Avoid general and meaningless job objectives. It's better to have none at all than to say, "A rewarding career in business with an opportunity for advancement." Yuk! It says nothing, and your resume goes on the reject pile unless your daddy owns the company.

Your Job Objectives

Plan on several; one for each copy of your resume. If you use a desktop publishing service or your own laser printer to do your resume, you can change the objective for every job you apply for. A good tactic is simply to insert the job title and company name that you are applying for as in the examples above.

   Write down your own objectives in the blanks provided.

OBJECTIVE: _____

OBJECTIVE: _____

OBJECTIVE: _____

OBJECTIVE: _____

OBJECTIVE: _____

OBJECTIVE: _____

OBJECTIVE: _____

Education   List your most recent degree, school, year of graduation, and major. If you studied overseas in a summer program, list the school and dates as well. Do not list the high school you attended unless (1) it is your highest degree or (2) it is prestigious and will be recognized by a potential employer. List your grade point average if it is over 3.0 on a 4.0 scale. If your major GPA is higher than a 3.0 but your cumulative GPA isn't, just list your major GPA. List significant course work if your career objective is not closely related to your major, or if you want to camouflage a weak GPA. Or, list projects that you did in classes that required the skills needed for the job (see example 3). If you graduated from college several years ago, list it last on the resume.

   Don't list the city and state your college is in unless it is an obscure town or the city name is needed to indicate which campus you attended such as State University of New York at Stony Brook.

Here are three examples of education statements:

Example 1

EDUCATION: Bachelor of Business Administration
University of Iowa, 1990
Major: Finance

GPA: 3.5 on 4.0 scale
Significant course work included:
Real Estate Financial Modeling, Practical Aspects of Working Capital Management,
Computer Modeling for Decision Making.

Example 2

EDUCATION: B.F.A. Visual Arts, University of Texas, Austin, 1987
Universite of Lausanne, Switzerland; one-year program, 1986
Art History, French, International Economics

Example 3

EDUCATION: B.B.A. Finance, University of Georgia, 1993
Major GPA: 3.6
Projects: Analytical study of financial structure of IBM corporation and subsidiaries.
Group leader of project.

Your Education

_____

_____

_____

_____

_____

_____

Educational or Other Achievements

Achievements show what you've accomplished. Review the skills list you compiled in the last chapter. What were the achievements for the skills you enjoyed using? For example, coordinating a class project in one of your courses and receiving an A is an achievement. Organizing a club activity and getting solid results can be an achievement. Even maintaining a 3.0 grade point average and working long hours on a part-time job is an achievement. Look at these examples and then write your own achievements. Focus on your strength and place your achievements in the upper two-thirds of the resume. Your achievements tell people who you are.

Some of your greatest achievements may not be things you can put on a resume, such as making it through college during your parents' divorce, overcoming an addiction, dealing with a difficult emotional situation, having the strength to seek counseling, overcoming depression and anxiety, or getting over a bad love affair. Sometimes just getting out of bed and getting on with your life is an achievement. Though these are not public achievements, they are truly significant maturing experiences, and they may have constituted your energy center during the last four years. Of course, these achievements don't go on the resume. Instead focus on your energy center or significant course work in the achievement section.

The achievement section is optional. It's a compact way to get across some major points about yourself. If your achievements were personal, skip achievements and go right to work experience.

Here are some examples of educational achievements:

ACHIEVEMENTS: Golden Key Honor Society
Phi Beta Kappa
Governor's Scholar
Selected from 100 students to participate in nation-wide M.B.A. competition.
Dean's list nine consecutive quarters

Remember, you don't have to have educational achievements. If your achievements were in work or activities, list them instead of educational achievements. Summarize and hit the highlights. Stress those activities where you succeeded or made a difference, especially as your achievement relates to the needs on the job.

Here are some examples of other achievements:

ACHIEVEMENTS: Worked full-time at night and maintained dean's list status for four years.

As academic chairman of Psi Psi Psi fraternity, established program to upgrade fraternity GPA. Program involved enforced quiet hours, and group-wide "hit the books" encouragement. Program helped raise group average from 2.5 to 3.1 in two years.

President of Alpha Kappa Psi Fraternity
- as president, initiated program to . . .
- supervised 10 committees that . . .

Coached 18 swim teams to national competition; record overall was 10 and 0

Produced 4 television programs that aired on public television.

Consistently received A's in calculus (if calculus relates to a job that requires analytical skills).

Paintings exhibited in four major shows including . . .

Won Poetry Award for best new poet from . . .

GRE score of . . . (*if it's high and your resume is for application to a grad school.*)

Organized Big Sister Chapter on campus that brought together 250 college students and underprivileged children.

Your Achievements

Skip if not applicable; go to work experience.

_____

_____

_____

_____

_____

_____

_____

_____

_____

_____

_____

_____

_____

_____

_____

_____

_____

_____

_____

_____

Work Experience Chances are, most of your college jobs have been part-time. You may even be embarrassed to list them. Don't be. No one expects you to have significant work experience at this point in your career. What recruiters are looking for is evidence of responsibility or leadership or intelligence. As a rule, recruiters don't seem to know what they are looking for, so we need to cover as many bases as possible.

Above all, be honest and use concrete examples. Never oversell your work. If you reorganized a plumbing supply truck, don't say you redesigned an inventory control system. It may be inventory, but your description makes it sound as if you did more than you really did.

If you have significant work experience, edit it to include the topics focused on below. Stress results, responsibility, and the contribution you made to the firm. Use short phrases and action verbs such as, "Organized student group to raise money for AIDS research."

You don't have to list every part-time or full-time job you've had in college. Focus on the jobs that demonstrate your skills best or are most closely linked with the skills required for the job. Concentrate on the following factors in each job to help you isolate the important qualities you demonstrated in your jobs.

Responsibilities

Results

Promotion

Improvements made

Skills used

Performance review

Keep the following in mind as you write your work experience:

1. List the job title, company, city, and dates. If the company is now well known, include some information; e.g., "A retail apparel sales store with $1 million in annual sales."

2. If you had specific responsibilities on the job, say what they were. Did you supervise anyone? How many? Did you assume the duties of the manager in his or her absence? How was the company better as a result of your working there? Stress results. Perhaps you took pressure off the manager by handling details—that's a result. Think!

3. How many hours a week did you work? This can be significant if you worked more than 20 hours per week during school or worked overtime during holidays and still maintained a grade point average of over 3.0. This also demonstrates your willingness to work. What percentage of your income did you earn? If it is 90 percent or 100 percent, list it.

4. Did you receive increasing responsibility on the job; for example, were you promoted from salad maker to head of wait staff at a restaurant?

5. Very important: How was the job evaluated? In other words, what was the behavior that made a successful employee in this job? For example, the goal might have been to expedite orders. If so, how well did you do it? How do you measure that performance? Sales or orders processed per hour or per day? If you are having difficulty evaluating your performance, consider how someone who did the job poorly did the job. How did your performance differ from his or hers?

6. Did you receive any awards? Employee of the month? What was the award based on? Service, responsibility? What skills did you use that would apply to the job you plan to interview for?

7. Were you given a formal performance review? If so, what did the employer especially like about you? Even if there wasn't a formal review, what did the employer say about you? Did the boss praise you for anything in particular? This is a clue to how people evaluate you. Were you consistent, accurate, prompt, a good manager, able to make the customers feel comfortable, a strong salesperson, a good organizer?

8. Remember, don't feel you must list every job. Some jobs just don't fit this formula. For those jobs, either list them by stating just the name and title or by grouping them under an umbrella:
   Part-time Bartender: Ray's Bar & Grill, Joe's Bar, 1998–2000.

9. For those you do list, stress achievements: promotion and objective praise, and performance review and skills noted in the review. Emphasize the skills required to do the job and the *results* of using those skills. Employers seem to be impressed with students who can understand the importance of achievements and results. Quantify the results, e.g., "painted 165 golf carts per day; sold $2,000 in jewelry per week."

Here are some examples of work experience. Note how in each of the examples, we focus on objective data on how the job was evaluated, skills, and results.

Bank Teller/First Trust
(dates)

Atlanta, Georgia.
Responsible for customer transactions as a floating teller in six branches.
- Based on performance at one branch, was promoted to travel team.
- Job performance review gave superior ratings for accuracy, ability to get along with others and customer service.
- Maintained 3.0 average; worked 32 hours per week during school year.

Intern Personnel Assistant/Bongo Manufacturing

(dates)   Tulsa, Oklahoma.

Responsible for screening applicants for recruiters during big recruitment drive for drum manufacturer with
$4 million in sales.

- Made detailed notes on applicants, which saved recruiters time.
- Processed applications and input data into computer
system.
- Succeeded in meeting the firm's need for employees
and completed the drive ahead of schedule.
- Management review praised work for identifying
quality applicants.

Gymnastics Coach/Omni Recreation

(dates)   Waukegan, Illinois.

- Taught gymnastics classes to all ages.
- Coached teams for competition and took care of ad-
ministrative details.
- Developed skills in communicating praise and in mo-
tivating team for high performance.
- Team won 90 percent of meets.

Sales Clerk/Diamonds To Go

(dates)   Pinkston, North Carolina.

Responsible for customer transactions/sales.

- Met sales quota and exceeded quota during busy holiday sales.
- Received employee-of-the-month award for outstanding sales.
- Showed ability to identify customer needs and sell
"big ticket" items (over $5,000).

Customer Service Clerk/Bigger Department Store

(dates)   Oleo, California.

Responsible for handling merchandise return and repair
counter.

- Job required tact and ability to calm irritable cus-
tomers.
- Processed orders quickly, which reduced waiting time
and irritability of customers.
- Promoted to head clerk; supervised 7 employees.
- Performance review gave superior ratings for tact and
management ability.
- Asked to join senior management training program.

Your Work Experience

(job title) _____

(dates of service) _____ (company name & city) _____

Responsibilities: _____

_____

Results: _____

_____

Promotion: _____

_____

Improvements made: _____

_____

Skills used: _____

_____

Performance review: _____

_____

_____

(job title) _____

(dates of service) _____ (company name & city) _____

Responsibilities: _____

_____

Results: _____

_____

Promotion: _____

_____

Improvements made: _____

_____

Skills used: _____

_____

Performance review: _____

_____

_____

(job title) _____

(dates of service) _____ (company name & city) _____

Responsibilities: _____

_____

Results: _____

_____

Promotion: _____

_____

Improvements made: _____

_____

Skills used: _____

_____

Performance review: _____

_____

_____

(job title) _____

(dates of service) _____ (company name & city) _____

Responsibilities: _____

_____

Results: _____

_____

Promotion: _____

_____

Improvements made: _____

_____

Skills used: _____

_____

Performance review: _____

_____

_____

Activities   You may have put your leadership activities in the achievement section. If not, place them under Activities. Emphasize how the organization was different as a result of your membership. What did you do or achieve, either as a group or as a leader?

How large is the organization? Were you elected or appointed to your office? If you don't have significant activities, you probably have a high grade point average or you have worked your way through school. If you have no activities, a low GPA and never had a part-time job, start thinking about a logical explanation for the low achievement. Don't feel bad about it, don't apologize to anyone. But you need to show the employer that you have come around and are now ready to get down to work. You may want to emphasize skills instead of activities. (See the next section.)

Here are some examples of activities:

ACTIVITIES: **Treasurer of Oga Pi Dodo**; responsible for $150,000 budget and collection of past dues. Set up collection system that recovered cash without creating hard feelings.

As Community Service chairman for Not A Bad Organization, organized a drinking awareness program.

- Created professionally produced bus cards to advertise goals of reduced drinking.
- Organized an awareness day that involved public safety officers and students; event was attended by 400 students.
- Arranged for McDLT to sponsor the event.
- Wrote press releases and arranged two nationally known speakers to attend.

Volunteer Disc Jockey/WOBO
Produced weekly radio program that achieved a 12% market share.
- Hired talent; substituted on air; produced commercials; wrote copy.

Your Activities

ACTIVITY 1: _____

_____

_____

_____

_____

ACTIVITY 2: _____

_____

_____

_____

_____

ACTIVITY 3: _____

_____

_____

_____

_____

Skills   You know your skills, but how do you put them on a resume and when do you do it? Use skills and examples in the following cases:

1. If you are applying for a job that requires certain skills, but your major and part-time jobs don't readily reveal your ability to do the job. For example, suppose you want a job as an interior decorator, but you majored in accounting and you worked only at fast-food restaurants. If you are interested in interior decorating, you must have done some designing or decorating, perhaps for your father's contracting firm or for your mother's bridge club:

   Skilled in designing work environments. Redesigned contracting firm's offices for efficiency and more congenial reception area.

2. When you want to impress the employer with your expertise in an area not covered in your work experience:

   Skilled in using Lotus 1–2–3 for real estate analysis.

3. When you feel your work experience, grade point average, and activities don't present a strong picture of you. Perhaps you spent most of your college years listening to your friends' problems, and the job you are seeking requires strong listening skills.

   Strong interpersonal communication skills; adept at intuiting others' problems and helping them come to a solution.

Your Skills

_____

_____

_____

_____

_____

_____

References

You don't need to list references on a resume. Prepare a list of names and addresses to take with you to the interview. Most employers don't check references until after they've talked to you.

A word about seeking references. If you are a student, choose only professors you know well. Ask them if they "feel comfortable" providing a letter of recommendation for you. That way, you don't put them on the spot. Often professors would rather not provide a reference but feel trapped by the student's request. If a professor agrees to provide a recommendation, supply him or her with your resume and transcript if possible. He or she needs something to go on. Otherwise, the professor will write something short, such as "this student was in the upper third of the class," which doesn't impress potential employers. Follow up to be sure your professors actually write the recommendation. Busy professors can be procrastinators.

If you are not a student, choose previous bosses and peers who know you well and have admired your performance.

Putting It All Together

Finally, let's take a look at some examples of completed resumes.

Resume Sample 1: Chronological

JOSEPH JONES

Current Address:
222 Campus Street
Campus City, Georgia 54444
(404) 555-5555

Permanent Address:
189 Golf Course Drive
Ritzy-Ritz, Georgia 55555
(404) 555-5555

OBJECTIVE: An entry-level position in real estate sales and analysis.

EDUCATION: Bachelor of Business Administration
University of Georgia; 1990
Major: Finance

GPA: 3.5 on a 4.0 scale
Significant course work included: Real Estate Financial Modeling, Practical Aspects of Working Capital Management, and Computer Modeling for Decision Making.

SKILLS: Skilled in using Lotus 1–2–3 for real estate analysis; strong selling ability

WORK EXPERIENCE:
Summer 1993

Sales Clerk/Diamonds To Go
Pinkston, North Carolina
Responsible for customer transactions and sales.
- Met sales quota and exceeded quota during busy holiday sales.
- Received employee of the month award for outstanding sales.
- Job required ability to identify customer needs and sell "big ticket" items (over $5,000).

Summer 1992

Customer Service Clerk/Bigger Department Store
Oleo, California
Responsible for handling merchandise return and repair counter.
- Job required tact and ability to calm irritable customers.
- Processed orders quickly, which reduced waiting time and irritability of customers.
- Promoted to head clerk; supervised 7 employees.
- Performance review gave superior ratings for tact and management ability.
- Asked to join senior management training program.

ACTIVITIES: As **Community Service Chairman** for Not A Bad Organization, developed a drug prevention program.
- Organized an awareness day that involved public safety officers and 400 students.
- Coordinated planning with law enforcement officers.

Resume Sample 2: Functional

JOSEPH JONES
189 Golf Course Drive
Ritzy-Ritz, Georgia 55555
(404) 555-5555

- Four years of part-time accounting experience in payables, receivable, and posting to general ledger at large manufacturing firm.
- Campus leadership as President of Sigma Tau Delta, an elected position in a 150-member fraternity.
- Maintained 3.4 average while working 30 hours per week part-time.
- Strong language skills: studied Spanish 6 years.
- Consistently received A's on research papers and analytical projects.

EDUCATION:
Bachelor of Arts in Literature.
University of Georgia; 1990

WORK EXPERIENCE:
Accounts Payable Clerk/Payroll Clerk 1986–1990
BULLDOG MANUFACTURING COMPANY

Maintained payroll for 400-employee company.
Responsible for monthly payables reconciliation.
- Revised system to produce more timely reports to corporate headquarters.
- Received raise, promotion; performance review gave superior ratings for ability to work well with others and initiative.
- Trained two employees on computer system.

ACTIVITIES:
President: Sigma Tau Delta
Established the first university-wide Greek Drug committee.
Increased membership by 50 percent through revised pledging activities.
Succeeded in collecting back dues without disrupting fraternity.
Raised $10,000 for leukemia through T-shirt sale fund-raiser.

Resume Worksheet

NAME

Current Address: **Permanent Address:**

_____   _____

_____   _____

phone: (   ) _____   phone: (   ) _____

OBJECTIVE: _____

EDUCATION: _____

                       _____

                       _____

                       _____

                       _____

EDUCATIONAL   (If your work experience is more significant, place it here instead.)
ACHIEVEMENTS
or OTHER   _____
ACHIEVEMENTS:
                       _____

                       _____

                       _____

                       _____

                       _____

                       _____

                       _____

                       _____

WORK EXPERIENCE: (job title) _____

                       If the company name is more significant, list it first.

(dates of service)   (company name & city) _____

                       Responsibilities: _____

                       _____

Results: _____

_____

Promotion: _____

_____

Improvements made: _____

_____

Skills used: _____

_____

Performance review: _____

_____

(job title) _____

If the company name is more significant, list it first.

(dates of service)   (company name & city) _____

Responsibilities: _____

_____

Results: _____

_____

Promotion: _____

_____

Improvements made: _____

_____

Skills used: _____

_____

Performance review: _____

_____

(job title) _____

If the company name is more significant, list it first.

(dates of service)   (company name & city) _____

Responsibilities: _____

_____

Results: _____

_____

Promotion: _____

_____

Improvements made: _____

_____

Skills used: _____

_____

Performance review: _____

_____

ACTIVITIES: (how you made the organization better)

_____

_____

_____

_____

_____

_____

SKILLS:

_____

_____

_____

_____

_____

_____

Resources for Putting Together Your Resume

- If you campus has a computer lab, especially one with Macintosh computers, type your resume there.

- If you hire someone, don't pay over $100, and ask about updating privileges.

- Check out Kinko's Copies. Some stores in this chain make a laser master and give you the disk. Whenever you want an update, just bring in the disk and they will make the changes for a small fee.

- Ask at the campus computer lab about people who will type and produce your resume for a small fee.

- Consider getting matching stationery and envelopes: small for thank-you notes and large for regular correspondence.

- Make a resume for each job you are applying for with the objective as the job title.

- Be wary of flamboyant resume styles. Ask to see a sample if you hire someone.

Have someone look at your resume and critique it, preferably someone in business and not the person you are interviewing with. Don't pay anyone for this. Better to have your uncle or someone in business look at it than a resume service.

Cover Letters That Sell

Along with your resume, you need to send a cover letter that highlights your potential contribution to the company. It's not a rehash of the resume, but a succinct description of what you offer the company. Before you write it, read ahead in the company research chapter to learn how to identify and understand the needs of the company.

Understanding the needs of the company puts you ahead of other letter writers. For example, if someone wrote you a letter trying to sell you aluminum siding when you live in an apartment, you would laugh and throw the letter away. Unfortunately, many resume cover letters do just that. They attempt to sell employers a product they don't need. So figure out their needs by reading the research chapter before you start.

Then forget everything you ever heard about letter writing. If you want to be noticed, do three things: (1) back up your qualifications with evidence; (2) rewrite and rewrite until you get a polished product; and (3) send the letter to the person who can hire you, not to the personnel department. Do not copy form letters out of books. Your feelings are not the same as those of writers of form letters. Why sound like a form letter?

Skip Ahead to the Research Chapter

If you are tempted to write a letter without having researched the company, you will regret it. But even if you are in a hurry, like most busy, impatient, and intelligent people, don't scribble something down and send it out without research. Without research, your letter may be vague, like the following:

> Personnel Department
> Mobil Oil Company
> City, State
>
> Dear Sir/Madam:
> I am a college senior majoring in business administration, and I would like to talk with you about a job with Mobil Oil. I would like to work for Mobil Oil Company because the company offers career opportunity and career growth. . . .

On first glance, this letter may sound acceptable. But think about it. The letter was sent to no one in particular. The reason the applicant wants to work for the company is career opportunity and growth, something most large firms should offer. The writer fails to name a specific occupational area he wants, which will leave the decision of where to direct the letter up to a personnel clerk who will probably file the letter on the bottom of the pile because he or she isn't sure what to do with it.

Instead of sending a vague letter, send a targeted letter. What do the most recent issues of *The Wall Street Journal* or *The New York Times* say about your company? Or, if it's a local or small company, what did you find out about the company in your research? How is the company you want to work for organized? What is its growth strategy? And how can you fit into that strategy? For example, if its growth strategy is to open up several new retail stores, and you want to work in that field, show why you are the most qualified. Highlight your experience and the fact that you may need less training than other candidates and have a solid employment record. Then point out how you increased sales and had no turnover and low absenteeism among the employees you managed in your part-time assistant manager's job in college. With those qualities, and evidence to back them up, you are sure to get an interview.

Or maybe you want a job as a stockbroker in training. You might point out in the letter that you already have a large pool of potential clients in a wealthy neighborhood of the city where the branch is located. You have shown that you know the ropes in the industry and are willing to put yourself on the line.

If it is a large company, look the company up in the *CPC Annual–A Guide to Employment Opportunities for College Graduates*, which is a directory of employment opportunities for college graduates. Here's an excerpt from the advertisement Mobil Oil Corporation uses (College Placement Council, *CPC Annual* (Bethlehem, PA: College Placement Council, Inc., 1987–88), Volume 3, p. 229):

> Mobil is looking for bright, imaginative men and women who enjoy working on difficult problems and getting things done . . . who thrive on challenge and aren't afraid of responsibility . . . who will try something new, even at the risk of failure. We're looking, in short, for a diverse group of people who can become the best in their fields—as we feel we're the best in ours.

If I were sending Mobil a letter, I would first find the correct division to send it to. The *CPC Annual* listing shows that Mobil is involved in five business lines: Exploration and production, marketing, refining, research and engineering, and chemical. I would then write the letter to emphasize the key areas the company wants.

Use concrete examples and results. Your letter might discuss consistency in finishing projects on or before a deadline and provide an example. It might describe difficult projects taken on and your success with them. Your high GPA would show commitment and intelligence. If you are a risk taker, dream up some examples of when you took risks and succeeded. You gathered most of your raw material in the chapter on skills.

Here is an example of a better cover letter:

Date

Name of director in charge of division you are interested in
Mobil Oil Company
City/State

Dear Mr. _____:

John Doe suggested I contact you about an entry-level position with the Engineering Department of Mobil Oil Company. I plan to graduate in June with a degree in Chemical Engineering from Purdue University.

Mobil is my first choice among potential employers because Mobil devotes more of its resources to research and development than any other oil company. I have also been impressed with the company's stability in times of volatile energy prices and its reputation for promotion from within.

I offer the company the skills and determination needed to make a strong contribution. My grade point average of 3.6 on a 4.0 scale places me in the top 25 percent of Purdue graduates. Since I have been in school, I have worked 30 hours per week as the night manager of a local pizza restaurant where I supervised the work of 15 employees nightly. I was fortunate to have worked with an owner who was willing to take risks and who allowed me to devise marketing programs to sell more pizza, each of which succeeded by surpassing our goal of increasing sales by 30 percent.

I will call next week to discuss a time to talk about a position with Mobil Oil Company.

Sincerely,

June Johnson

Do your best to get a contact within the company who will hand deliver your letter to the manager in charge of the area you are interested in. If you must go in cold, send the letter to the person who has the power to hire you.

Notice that the writer shows evidence of skills and accomplishments that are important for this job. The writer uses a contact and says in the first line what he or she wants. Whenever you ask for something in a letter, say what you want up front and be specific. Then tell the company why you are interested in the job. Next say why you are the best person for the job using evidence. Finally, suggest a method for arranging to meet, such as, "I will be in New York during the week of May 15; I will call to see if we can find a convenient time to meet."

Keep in mind that this letter was only an example to show you how you must tailor your letter to the company's needs. Someone in the chemical division may have no idea what the personnel division said it wants in employees. The chemical division boss may not know what you are talking about if you write that you are a risk taker. That person may not even like risk takers. So, whenever possible, be sure that you tailor your letter to the person who wrote the advertisement.

To Whom Do You Send the Cover Letter?

Is the job you want under the vice president for marketing or the vice president for administration? Unfortunately, you are going to have to find this out through a company contact. When I called a large company's personnel offices to find out information on entry-level jobs, I didn't get to speak with anyone, only with their voice mail. My phone calls were not returned. I suggest finding a real person, a contact within who will help you figure out the company. Your contact should know someone in the company and be able to help you get your letter and resume into the right hands.

Find out the name of the person who has the power to hire you and send your letter directly to him or her. Do this by calling the company switchboard and asking for the department that is offering the job. Ask the secretary in the department whom correspondence concerning the position should be directed to. Be sure to get the spelling of the name and the title right. She might say all applications are being taken by the personnel director. It may be company policy that the personnel department screens all applicants. If that is the case, go ahead and send it to the personnel department—but why not send a copy to the boss, too?

Never do a broad-scale mailing directed just to personnel departments. Whenever possible, send your resume and personalized cover letter directly to your potential boss, or have your contact pass it to the boss.

If you live close enough, walk your resume and letter around. Don't expect anyone to talk with you, but let them see you. Drop your letter off and say you will call back for an appointment. Dress as you would for the interview.

If you know anyone in the company, let him or her know you will be interviewing with the company and pump your contact for information. If your contact can help you get an interview, take advantage of that help. Follow up with a thank-you note emphasizing what you discussed and expressing appreciation and an offer to be of service to him or her in the future.

Obviously, make sure your letter is typed on high-quality bond without messy corrections.

Here is a standard format for a business letter:

                                                    Street Address
                                                    City, State, Zip
                                                    Date

(four spaces)

Name
Title
Company
Street Address
City, State, Zip
   (two spaces)

Dear Ms./Mr. _____*: (address all letters to a specific person)*
   (two spaces)

   John Brown contacted me last week to tell me about a job you have available in your chemical weapons division. I am especially interested since I majored in chemistry and became a commander in the campus ROTC before joining the chemical weapons division of the U.S. Army. I believe my training in defoliants and other chemical warfare serums will prove a valuable addition to your department.

   I will contact you next week. Perhaps we could then set up a convenient time to discuss the position and your company's needs in this area.
(two spaces)

                                                    Sincerely,

                                                    (four spaces)
                                                    Your name

(two spaces)

Enclosure (if you are enclosing something)

Company Risk

How to Research Large Companies

The biggest mistake students make is not knowing what they have to offer. The second biggest mistake is not bothering to understand the needs and problems of the industry and employer.

Everyone advises you to research the company, but no one ever tells you how. Business students sometimes have an advantage in understanding how to evaluate a company, but even they don't really know where to look or what to look for.

The Big Don't   Don't figure you can spend 15 minutes before the interview glancing at the annual report and then be able to talk intelligently about the company. Recruiters can spot the quick-scan candidate and will look for candidates who are better prepared.

Think about the people you are competing with for the job. If you are a graduating college senior, your competition has, aside from different grade point averages, probably at least the same part-time work and extracurricular experience you have, if not more—perhaps much more.

Recently, one of my students went up against a college superstar for a job with a large corporation. The superstar had an impressive GPA, belonged to several honor societies, and was vice president of the student government. My student had never joined a club and had a much lower GPA than the superstar. He knew he had to make a good impression to overcome his considerably slimmer credentials. He decided to learn everything he could about the company by following the steps outlined in this chapter. He didn't use everything he knew in the interviews, but he knew about the most recent changes in the product line, and he knew the background and management style of the CEO.

The interviewer was impressed that the student had taken the time to really understand the company. The superstar, on the other hand, breezed into the interview expecting to get the job based on her outstanding college performance. The superstar didn't get the job, but the student who had researched the company did.

According to the University of Georgia Career Planning and Placement Center, for every 20 students who interview for a job, four are invited for a second interview, and two actually get offers. The competition is intense, and research gives you a leg up on the competition. It also helps you spot the companies who pose the greatest risk of unemployment in the near future.

How Long Does It Take to Research a Company?

Think about it this way. How much time would you spend in choosing a car? Would you look it up in *Car and Driver* and *Consumer Reports*? Would you check all the dealers? How long would that take? A job is a much bigger investment than a car. The research you do on the company might never come up in the interview, but you need to have a firm grip on what the company does and what your prospects are.

Plan to spend an hour or two per company. If you are interviewing with several companies, speed up the process by looking up several at the same time. Devote as least as much time to looking into the company as you would preparing for an exam. After all, this is your life, not just a grade.

What Are You Really Trying to Find Out?

First, you want to know exactly how the company makes money. Even if you don't plan to work for the company for the rest of your life, you probably will want to work there for a couple of years—at least until you pay off your college loan or new car. If you don't know how the company makes money, you won't know how secure your job is.

Job seekers often assume that since they have heard of the company, it's a good company to work for. This strategy fails to take into account the basics. What's the product? What are the possibilities for growth? What are the risks? What are the possibilities for a hostile takeover or layoffs? How would a change in ownership of the company affect your job security and chances for a raise?

You as an up-and-coming executive may not be worried about job security. You may think if you are smart enough and work hard enough you will float to the top like cream no matter what happens to your company. Right? Maybe. Maybe not.

International competition, shareholders' demands, inflation, recession—all of these factors have beat up U.S. companies pretty badly. Good, hardworking, experienced people have been let go. New hires, like you, have been let go. It's time to take care of yourself, look out for yourself, and find out everything you can about potential employers. Not because they are the bad guys who could fire you, but because the shoves companies are taking in the marketplace could shove you back on the street.

A company's fortunes can change rapidly, and even the best of research programs can't always foretell disaster. That's why research is important—not just research on whether you will like the job, but research on whether the job will still be there tomorrow. Here's a case in point: General Dynamics fired 3,318 employees who were working on the top-secret Navy A-12 attack aircraft at a plant in Texas a few years ago. The U.S. Secretary of Defense cancelled the project, and within 24 hours more than 3,000 people, many of whom made $35,000 to $40,000 per year, were out of a job.

Should the A-12 cutback have come as a surprise? Not to prospective employees who did their homework. As early as December 1990, *U.S. Industrial Outlook*, a one-volume reference book available at large libraries, predicted the downturn of the defense industry and the likelihood of cutbacks. In 1992, less than two years after the A-12 cutbacks, *The Wall Street Journal* reported General Dynamics announced plans to sell three operations: missile, materials, and commercial aircraft. These businesses represented 20 percent of the company's sales. The writing was on the wall in 1990, yet despite the availability of this information, job seekers tend to overlook it or rely on assurances by company recruiters instead of checking out the industry for themselves. The industry affects the fortunes of the company in a big way.

The A-12 helicopter was a high-risk, high-return project. General Dynamics' problem came from having only one major project. When that project went belly up, the entire project staff went out the door. When the defense industry as a whole declined after the fall of the Soviet Union, the missile division was put on the block. Whenever you work for a company that depends on one group of customers to buy its product, you face unemployment risk. And it's not just in the defense industry. The same can be true of an advertising agency that has only one major client or a job with a nonprofit agency that gets funding from only one source. It can also be true of government jobs in states that have budget-balancing laws.

Less than a year after the Pentagon cancelled the A-12, the United States fought and won the war with Iraq, watched the fall of the Soviet Union, and began making plans to spend the "peace dividend." Yet in this hostile environment for defense spending, General Dynamics was ranked favorably by investment advisors because it was well managed and, they thought, could survive the troubled times better than other defense contractors. The company was praised by investment advisors because it generated cash even in tough times. We know how it generated some of its cash: by cutting employees as it cut projects. This makes business sense, of course, but would you want to work for a company where you could be on the street with 24 hours' notice?

How stable is your prospective employer? Consider these three factors:

1. The financial stability of the customers who pay for the company's product has a significant impact on your employment security. If the people buying your company's product suddenly don't have any money to spend, or stop buying it for some other reason, you could be at risk if most of the company's money comes only from those people.

2. The swings of political climate can affect your employment—defense contracts or the lack of regulation of your industry, free-spending vs. tight-fisted government administrations.

3. How well managed the company is affects your employment risk; from an investor's point of view, a well-managed company may act more quickly to cut jobs. A well-managed company from an employee's point of view may be less risky and generate just as high returns.

Takeover Risk and What It Can Mean to You

In the 1980s hostile takeovers and mergers became fashionable. Companies began concentrating on what they did best, their core businesses, and they eliminated businesses that didn't fit with the core. They also took over other companies that provided a strategic or cash flow advantage. They paid for these acquisitions with junk bonds.

While the takeover movement has died down in the 1990s, you will understand more about business if you understand how it came about in the first place. Not all takeovers are bad. Some can actually stabilize a company. For example, if you own a campus ice cream stand, and you decide to buy a year-round tee-shirt business to supplement your income, you are stabilizing your cash flow. You will have income all year long, not just during the hot months when ice cream sales are strong. Or, you may make a strategic acquisition by buying a company that can supply your ice cream more profitably. To make these acquisitions, you will borrow some money; that's your debt. If sales increase, you will easily be able to make your payments. But if sales don't increase, and principal payments on debt must continue, you could be in trouble.

Similarly, in the corporate world, takeovers can ultimately make companies more secure by stabilizing cash flows, or they can impoverish them by strangling them with debt. For example, if your company takes over a company with stable cash flows—such as a food company, which is often resistant to recessionary ups and downs (even in bad times, people eat)—then your company has more flexibility. If your company buys a company with the technology to expand into a new market, your company may ultimately spend less on the acquisition than it would have spent trying to develop the technology itself. On the other hand, if the expansion doesn't pay off in increased sales, there's no money to pay the debt.

Some companies came out of the takeover days healthier and leaner. Some took on too much debt, and despite the low interest rates in the early 1990s, they went under with the recession or had to renegotiate the terms of their loans. The recession reduced how much money consumers had to spend, which in turn depressed sales. When sales are down and debt is up, someone has to pay the price. To reduce costs, employees were fired at some companies. But if the cutting came from divisions that were not profitable anyway, the takeover just speeded up the process.

What you want to consider are the kinds of gambles your company is making and if the company has enough of a cash cushion to prevent a major shake-up in your life as an employee. Or, if your company takes over another company and spends every spare dime buying it out, where does that put you? Unfortunately, it may put you out of a job as a recent hire, or it might mean that you work 15 hours a day, because the company's profit margins are cut so thin that it has three people doing the work of 10.

Takeovers can do your career some good if you are at the right place. If you work for a company undergoing these changes, you may be spared from termination because of your low income as a new employee. In this case, you may get to handle more responsibility sooner and get more recognition for what to do. People a few levels above your own may be cut, allowing you to see the top of the business more clearly. You may say good-bye to your friends working in the less profitable divisions of the company, which often are sold off to finance the acquisition. Your friends in the less profitable division face a potentially less pleasant fate back on the street looking for another job. Our goal is to be sure you are not one of them.

A recent study found more white-collar workers were laid off during takeovers than blue-collar workers, and layoffs were more likely when the takeover was uninvited. Theoretically, when companies are sold to companies in the same industry, employees who have gone out of their way to do good work or become noticed could be spared the ax, but no studies confirm this conjecture.

Unfortunately for many workers, the ax will continue to fall in the 1990s. Besides restructurings and takeovers, companies will continue to downsize. Fewer workers will be needed. The companies that have already gone through the layoffs will be a better bet than those just waking up to the fact that they cannot compete with leaner companies.

It is crucial that you read *The Wall Street Journal* or *The New York Times* daily if you plan to interview with a major company. Though the crash-research program outlined here is pretty good, there is no substitute for really understanding the players and how the economy can affect your company. The only smart way to keep up with this is by reading a major newspaper. Local papers will not provide you with a broad enough perspective on large companies. (Local papers can provide useful information on local businesses and on the likelihood of budget cutbacks at state-funded agencies, however.)

Through your contacts, you have identified several potential employers. You may have signed up for campus interviews with some and plan to contact others on your own. To find out about large companies and subsidiaries of large companies, you must first know the name of the parent company. If you are unsure about the parent's name, check the library for *Who Owns Whom* or *America's Corporate Families: The Billion Dollar Directory* or *Standard & Poor's Register of Corporations, Directors and Executives.* Also check the computer-based *Disclosure* (sometimes known as *Compact Disclosure* or *Corporate Disclosure*) which will allow you to search through 10,000 publicly held companies for your division.

The Eight Must-Knows for Large Companies

1. The company's best-selling products.

2. The industry: opportunities and threats.

3. The company's growth strategy.

4. The company's financial condition.

5. The company's chief competitors and market position.

6. The CEO's background and management style.

7. What you offer the company. What need can you fill?

8. Why you want to work for this company.

1. The Company's Best-Selling Products

How is the company making money? What is the product that hauls in the *most* loot? Is it toothpaste or mining equipment or travel services or chocolate-chip cookies?

You need to know the profitable product lines for three reasons:

- To avoid the flat-out embarrassment of being caught off guard in the interview. Believe it or not, some job seekers go into interviews without knowing this crucial information.

- To determine whether you are going into the most profitable division of the company. Losing divisions often are the first to lose employees when cutbacks come. Winning divisions are the company's "favored children" and may provide you with the greatest career growth.

- To analyze the long-term prospects of the company. You must know the long-range prospects of the best-selling product line.

On the income statement, the different businesses or product lines will be listed under Gross Income. You can quickly see which is the biggest number, and you can see the five-year trend. Here is an an example from an annual report:

GROSS INCOME	**1989**	**1990**	**1991**	**1992**
Railcar Leasing and Management	$226.8	$215.9	$217.9	$233.3
Financial Services	101.0	104.0	125.0	128.0

You can tell pretty quickly that this company makes most of its money from railcar leasing and management. But notice the growth in financial services. That's significant, too. You might ask an interviewer about this and ask whether more emphasis is going to be put on financial services since they have been growing steadily in recent years. If you are being hired for a division that's not doing well, you naturally want to determine its plan for turning things around. Otherwise, when the sell-off starts, it could be you on the block with the company.

During the 1980s, companies loaded up on extra divisions, such as financial services companies, in the conglomerate/takeover binge. Now even the winning divisions acquired during the 1980s are at risk. For example, Sears recently announced it would sell its financial services unit, E.F. Hutton. The retailer said it would concentrate on its core business—retailing.

What does all this mean? The safest job may be with a company that has already downsized, in either a profitable division or a division that is part of the company's core business.

Use *The Wall Street Journal Index*, the library's Infotrac computer search system, or *Reader's Guide to Periodical Literature* (there is a version for business) for articles on the company. Especially note new products introduced and strategies announced.

New products can tell you about the company's growth prospects. One student applying for a financial position with a paper firm learned more about diapers and market placement of diapers than he ever thought he would short of fatherhood. While the rest of the students were out partying, he was reading up on diaper marketing to understand the company's introduction of a new product. He was well informed when he went into the interview; he impressed the interviewer and got the job.

2. The Industry: Opportunities and Threats

Let's say you wanted to look at the defense contracting industry because you have a job interview with General Dynamics for a position as a cost accountant. You may mistakenly think that since you are interviewing for an accounting position, you don't need to know about the company's product line and the problems of the industry. Wrong. The company makes its money selling products. Selling products pays your salary. Everything that happens to your company affects your future.

Whether you are looking for a small company or a large one, determine which industry makes your company the *most* money. The company may be an oil refiner that also has a plastics division. If it makes most of its money refining oil, look up oil refining in the *U.S. Industrial Outlook* (available at libraries). In a couple of pages you'll get a clear view of the problems the industry faces. You will not only be better prepared for the interview, you also will have a basis for evaluating other companies operating in that industry.

How do you find out what industry the company operates in? If you are not sure, a good place to start is with the company's primary SIC (standard industrial code). SICs cover everything from Industrial Inorganic Chemicals to Retail Grocery Stores. There are code numbers for big categories of industries and small, such as Greeting Card Publishing, Periodicals Publishing & Printing, Service Industries, etc. Many companies have several codes. Find out what the company calls its *primary* SIC. The SIC will be listed in *The Million Dollar Directory*, the computer-based *Disclosure* and *S&P Reports*. If the company is too small to be listed in one of these directories, find out what product makes the most money and look up that industry in *U.S. Industrial Outlook*.

Predicast's Basebook lists the industry's projected growth rate and number of employees by SIC number. Notice whether the industry as a whole is growing or shrinking.

The SIC code will be useful when you can't find information about the company from the usual sources. For example, if the company is owned by a foreign conglomerate, the company often will not be listed in the standard reference books. Using the SIC code, you can look up the industry by number and get a feeling for the type of business the company is engaged in. You can then check *Standard & Poor's Industry Surveys* or *U.S. Industrial Outlook* for information on the industry.

The managers who interview you will like you better if you understand the company and industry. And you will be able to decide whether their company is too risky if you know about the risk affecting the entire industry as well as the company. For example, if the price of oil goes up, all the industries that depend on oil and its by-products are affected. Once you understand how certain factors affect an entire industry, you can assess your company's risks. If your company has been taking a beating in the stock market, but all the other companies in that industry have as well, then you know you need to do more digging on your individual company. It may be a good company with a promising future after all.

For other good industry overviews, check the January issues of *Forbes* or *Fortune*. Also check *Value Line Standard & Poor's Industry Surveys* (ask the reference librarian where to find it). You often will uncover problems that plague the entire industry, and therefore your potential employer.

Check the financial ratios of the industry and compare your company to the industry by checking the *Almanac of Business and Industrial Financial Ratios* and *Industry Norms and Key Business Ratios*. That way you can determine what is normal performance for the industry in order to better compare your company's performance. Ratios are not complicated or confusing. They are simply a quick way to express the relationship between various parts of the balance sheet. For now, photocopy the industry ratios that apply to your industry for comparison later. Generally, there are industry averages for earnings and sales. How does your company compare? Is it at the top or the bottom of the industry? Why? If it's an insurance company, look in *Best's Key Rating Guide: Property Casualty* (insurance company rating guide) for a rating and description of the firm.

Almost every industry has trade journals. These magazines and newspapers, written exclusively for the industry, include regional trade publications, such as *Poultry Times* for the poultry industry, and national trade news, such as *The American Banker*. Ask the librarian about trade journals for your industry. You will be surprised at what good information you get about the industry that will put you ahead in the interviewing game. For example, you may learn about new trends in product or services. Trade journals may publish a profile of the executive whose division you are interviewing with, or they may fill you in on the biggest problems facing the industry.

3. The Company's Growth Strategy

How does your company plan to get bigger? Or get smaller? How does it plan to make more money? Does your company want to move into a new product area like computers or waste management? If it is a bank, does it want to be a small-town bank or does it want to be a bank that lends money to business? Does your company want to get rid of all of its businesses except chemical products? What does it say it wants to do?

Wall Street Journal articles will reveal strategy. For example, in the early 1990s, Wal-Mart became such a big force in retailing that Kmart was forced to invest millions of dollars in upgrading its stores to look like Wal-Mart. *The Wall Street Journal* carried several articles on how consumers reacted to the new Kmart.

How has Kmart's stock price been doing since it announced the big capital expenditures and restructuring? That's how you can tell whether the market thinks the company will generate profits in the future. But you can't look at one day's stock price to determine this; instead look at the price over the last three years. Look at earnings. Are they going up? *Value Line* will tell you what the market thinks about the company's strategy.

How to use 10Ks. Every company that sells stock must submit its dirty laundry to the Securities and Exchange Commission in a document called a 10-K. The 10K lists both positive and negative information about the company. Annual reports generally list only positive information. By reading the 10K form, you can find out who the officers are and how much they get paid, recent company lawsuits, problems, competitors, suppliers, and customers. Sometimes you can also learn about its growth strategy or what it considers its market niche.

To get a copy of the 10K form, write or call the company's investor relations department (sometimes called shareholder services) and request it. They will mail it to you, no questions asked. Also ask for a copy of the annual report.

Let's say you are interviewing with a wood products company that makes the most of its money by selling to companies that build houses. Here's what the 10K of one wood products firm recently said:

> The Corporation's sales and cash flows are affected by changing economic conditions in the markets which it serves. The Corporation's building products business is affected by the level of housing starts, the level of the availability, and cost of mortgage funds. Demand for pulp and paper products correlates closely with real growth in the gross national product, but is also affected by industry productive capacity, currency exchange rates and foreign market conditions.

Boring, right? Take a closer look. The company provides clues to its strategy and weaknesses in the statement above. It says the construction and home building industry affect sales. When interest rates are not favorable or when there is an economic recession, there is less building; therefore, the company faces a reduction in sales.

The construction industry is one of the most sensitive to swings in the economy. Companies that depend exclusively on construction can reap big rewards in boom times and face big losses in hard times. The company's annual report shows it recently took over a facial-tissue company. Even during a recession, people need something to blow their noses on. Hence the acquisition.

What's the risk with this company? In a recessionary economy there's less mortgage money to go around. Therefore, even though the company has made moves to stablilize its cash flows and depend less on the wildly fluctuating construction market, the company didn't get the new company for nothing. It may have taken on debt.

From the company's statements, you can also see that the company is selling its products abroad. Is its strategy to stabilize income by selling abroad? Companies with a foothold in the growing world markets should do better than those that don't. If they can sell enough abroad and make enough on paper products, they may offset the downturn in the building products industry. But will the debt burden the company may have taken on to acquire the tissue company force serious cutbacks of staff if interest rates suddenly change and make their debt payments too high? I would ask about this in an interview—in a subtle way, of course.

Ask the recruiter, in as tactful and as friendly a way as possible, if your perception of the company's strategy was right, and what risks he or she believes the strategy would pose to entry-level employees and their promotions, raises, and work loads. Will the company continue to focus on building products in the future? What was the reasoning behind the acquisition of the facial-tissue company?

The 10K report will also tell you if the price of the company's raw material is stable. Companies can get in a bind when the price of their raw materials shoots up and the market they sell to suddenly has less cash to spend. That's why it's important to know whom the company sells to and what raw materials go into the product. The 10K will usually tell you both.

But more important than anything is the market. Are people buying the product? If not, why?

4. The Company's Financial Condition

Even if you have never looked at a balance sheet, look at net sales (or net revenues) in the annual report or *Disclosure*. Are they going up? How about debt? To figure out how much debt it has, divide long-term liabilities by stockholder's equity. That's the debt-to-equity ratio. If it's high, the company has taken on a lot of debt.

What's the problem with that? In fact, it's okay to take on a lot of debt if you also have low operating leverage and/or high sales. But a lot of debt and declining sales don't augur well for the company. It could mean a lot of cost-cutting and long hours on the job because the company doesn't hire enough people to do the work. On the other hand, a "growth company" may be on the verge of something big and have both significant debt and low sales as a result. So, how do you tell the difference? More research. Comb *The Wall Street Journal Index* for articles about your company.

Some companies came out of the 1980s debt-free. Dreyfus, Dun & Bradstreet, Family Dollar Stores, Florida East Coast Industries, Tambrands, and Tootsie Roll had no long-term debt on their balance sheets during the early 1990s. When a cash crunch comes at one of these companies, it will have the money or access to the money to meet cash requirements. And chances are better that your job will not be sacrificed.

This is not to say that you should necessarily fear debt. Debt offers companies tax advantages and the chance to invest in new growth opportunities when cash is short. Some companies with low or no debt may have extra cash on hand because they don't have any great ideas on what to invest in to make more money. Or maybe the company wants to stay debt-free to take advantage of opportunities when they come along.

Even small firms produce an annual report. To understand what the earnings numbers mean, Baruch Lev, an accounting professor at the University of California at Berkeley, suggests several strategies for uncovering the truth in a company's financial statements.

First, he suggests comparing the finished goods inventory with the sales (revenue) by comparing the growth rates of each. He says that companies can hide negative information in earnings numbers, but this comparison of growth rates reveals the firm's true position. Get your calculator ready and turn to the annual report financial statements.

Look at the annual report under "finished goods." Compare the growth of the finished goods from last year to this year. Then turn to the page that lists the net revenue and compare the growth from last year. (Sales and revenue are terms used interchangeably.) Here's an example:

Consolidated Financial Statements
(In millions of dollars, except per-share amounts)

For the years ended December 31

Income	1990	1991
Net revenues	$6,567	$6,784

To calculate growth in net revenues, subtract $6,567 from $6,784 which equals $217. Divide $217 by $6,567 to find growth of .03 or 3 percent.

Now compare that number with the growth of finished goods in the inventory:

Inventories

	Millions of Dollars	
	1990	**1991**
Finished Goods	$815	$887

When you subtract last year from this year and divide to find the growth rate as above, you see the company's inventory grew by 9 percent while sales grew only by 3 percent. That means people aren't buying as fast as the company produces. Not a good sign.

Next look at total operating costs and expenses and compare the growth in expenses with the growth in revenues.

	1990	**1991**	
Net revenues	$6,567	$6,784	+3%
Total operating costs and expenses	6,593	7,033	+7%

As you can see, expenses are growing faster than sales. Eventually, the company will have to either increase sales or cut expenses. And since it's easier to cuts expenses than increase sales, this company may cut jobs to improve earnings.

Auditors from an accounting firm are responsible for verifying that a company's financial statements reflect the true condition of the firm's finances.

If the accounting firm does not write an opinion, or "qualifies" its opinion, which means it is saying that it can't stand behind all of the numbers, this information should be a red flag that the numbers you see in the annual report are not accurate or misleading. The auditor's opinion should say, "In our opinion, the consolidated financial statements referred to above fairly, in all material respects, reflect the financial position of X firm in the years . . ." If the annual report does not include such a statement, watch out.

If the company sells stock on one of the smaller stock exchanges, it may not be listed in the big directories, but information may be available in one of the following sources:

- *NASDAQ Fact Book & Company Directory.* Check this reference for addresses, phone numbers, stock symbol, and one-year price history. If it's not at your library, you can order it from the National Association of Securities Dealers, Finance Department, 9513 Key West Avenue, Rockville, MD 20850.

- *American Stock Exchange Fact Book.* Similar to the *NASDAQ Fact Book*, it costs $10 and can be ordered from American Stock Exchange Publications Department, 86 Trinity Place, New York, NY 10004.

- *Moody's Handbook of OTC Stocks* provides brief company profiles, financial data, earnings, history, and contacts. Check libraries.

- *Standard & Poor's Over-The-Counter Stock Reports* lists individual information on 1,600 companies whose shares of stock are traded over the counter. Check libraries for this valuable source on small companies.

What does the future hold for your company? Who has the best guess on the company's future prospects? If the company sells stock to the public, the stock price reflects what experts think about the company's future prospects. The balance sheet in the annual report provides useful information about past growth, but you want to know about the company's prospects in the future.

Securities analysts constantly monitor what publicly traded companies do. They look at management, product lines, the competition, and economic conditions to find securities that will grow in value or produce healthy earnings. Earnings, or net income, are the profit a company has after it has paid its expenses. The usual way investors evaluate a company's future is by calculating the ratio of the company's stock price to earnings for each share of stock the company has outstanding. Called the PE (price-to-earnings) ratio, this calculation helps investors compare companies within an industry. A large PE ratio may mean the stock market is willing to pay a higher price for the stock because the market believes the company has more growth opportunities.

The PE ratio is listed in the newspaper where stock price quotations are. The current stock price tells you what the market thinks of the company's future prospects. In general, a company the market expects to have a profitable future has a higher stock price. The earnings per share tell how the company has done recently. If you know, for example, that your company's PE ratio is 25 and its next closest competitor (in the same industry) is 30, then the company with a PE of 30 may have better growth prospects.

To find the company's stock price, look in the financial section of a major newspaper. Stock prices are quoted on three exchanges: the New York Stock Exchange, the American Stock Exchange and the NASDAQ National Market Issues. The larger companies typically trade on the New York Stock Exchange. Look across the top of the page.

NEW YORK STOCK EXCHANGE COMPOSITE TRANSACTIONS

52 Weeks											
Hi	Lo	Stock	Sym	Div	%	PE	Vol 100s	Hi	Lo	Close	Net Chng
66¾	37⅛	Tyco Labs	TYC	.36	.8	15	2508	45	42¼	45	+⅝

Here's what these numbers mean:

- The first numbers for the New York Stock Exchange are the "52 week Hi and Lo." That tells you the highest and lowest prices the stock has traded at in the last year.

- "Stock" tells the name of the company. Usually it is abbreviated.

- "Sym" is the way the exchange abbreviates the name.

- "Div" tells what the annual dividend payment per share is. In this case it's 36 cents.

- "Percent yield" is how much an investor can expect as a return on each share of stock at the current price.

- "PE" is the price-earnings ratio, which gives you an idea of what the market thinks about your firm. The stock in the example is trading at 15 times earnings. If you saw that the PE of the closest competitor was 20, you would want to do a little digging to find out why the market thinks the competitor will generate better earnings in the future. The PE can be valuable when you are comparing established firms in the same industry. If your company is a start-up company, there is not enough earnings history or information about future performance for it to have a useful PE ratio.

- "Vol" tells you how many lots of 100 shares traded that day.

- "Hi," "Lo," and "Close" are the prices the stock traded at that day.

- "Chng" is the dollar amount of the change since yesterday.

How do people rate the financial health of your company? *Standard & Poor's Register of Corporations, Directors and Executives* and *Moody's Investors Services* (both available at libraries) rate your company's debt. If a large amount of your company's debt is rated BA or lower, it is considered speculative-grade debt, and riskier than investment-grade debt. How well is the company doing in sales? Remember, a heavy load of debt that is rated risky (in terms of the company's ability to repay its debts) and low sales or high operating costs signal an unpleasant future.

5. The Company's Chief Competitors and Market Position

Who else is making toothpaste or mining equipment? How well are they doing? Are they ahead of your company? Why? To understand how secure your company is, you need to know whom they compete with. This information helps you determine how risky the company is. For example, if your company is on the bottom of the list of mining equipment manufacturers, it may go out of business. You certainly would want to know why it is on the bottom and if it has a plan to move up.

Use the computer search system at your library (*Disclosure* or *CD Corporate*) to find other companies with the same SIC numbers as your company. In general, how are these other companies doing? Read or print out the quick profiles on the other companies with the same SIC number. If your company has several SICs, look at the industry you are interviewing with and compare its competitors. For example, if you are interviewing with the mining division, look up other mining companies by searching for the mining SIC.

Here's an example of a small part of a report on Rockwell International Corporation from *Disclosure*:

ROCKWELL INTERNATIONAL CORP
2230 East Imperial Highway
El Segundo, CA 90245

Telephone: 310-797-3311
Disclosure No.: R721350000
Cross Reference: Was North American Rockwell Corp.

Incorporation: DE (*This indicates the firm was incorporated in Delaware, a state many firms choose for incorporation due to its friendly business laws.*)
Exchange: NYS

Ticker Symbol: ROC (*This is the abbreviated name of the company used in stock-price quotations.*)

Fortune No.: 0020
Forbes No.: SA040; AS101, PRO51; MV070
CUSIP No.: 0007743471
DUNS (TM) No.: 00 025 5523 (*Dun & Bradstreet produces reports on companies. If you know someone who has access to D&B, key in the DUNS number for a report. Some libraries offer this service for a fee.*)

PRIMARY SIC CODE:

3721: Aircraft
SIC CODES:
3721: Aircraft
3761: Guided Missiles and Space Vehicles
3764: Space Propulsion Units and Parts
3002: Radio and TV Communication Equipment
3714: Motor Vehicle Parts and Accessories
3555: Printing Trades Machinery

Description of Business: Engaged in research and development, manufacturing, and sale of manned and unmanned space systems, rocket engines, aero structures and military aircraft, defense electronics systems and products, avionics, telecommunications, micro electronics systems and equipment; also development, manufacture and market of heavy duty trucks and other vehicles, flow control and distribution production, high speed presses and related graphic arts equipment, industrial sewing machines and power tools.

The *Disclosure* report goes on to report annual sales, the most profitable business line, earnings growth, how the company does compared with the industry, who owns the company, the number of employees, and the company's balance sheet information.

Notice the *Disclosure* report also lists the identification numbers for *Forbes, Fortune,* and *DUNS.* These analyses and listings will give you more information.

If your library doesn't have *Disclosure*, photocopy the page on your company from *Standard & Poor's Register of Corporations, Directors and Executives*. Jot down the names of the CEO, the primary businesses the company is in and the company's primary SIC code.

To get a good look at the competition in your company's primary industry, use *The Million Dollar Directory*. The following listing of companies by rank within the same SIC code in the Aircraft and Parts Industry (SIC 372) comes from *The Million Dollar Directory*. Notice which company is on top, which is in the middle, and which is on the bottom. Why do you think GE is the biggest? Does that make it the best? Not necessarily. But before you interview with the Aircraft and Parts Division, you had better know why your company is number one or number seven. You also want to know how it plans to become number one.

AIRCRAFT AND PARTS (partial list)
INCLUDES SIC (S) 372

Company*	Sales (000)	Rank	Employees No.	Rank	Employees at this location	Primary SIC	Stock ticker symbol
General Electric	50,100,000	1	298,000	1	550	3724	GE
United Techs Corp.	18,000,000	2	187,000	2	475	3724	UTX
The Boeing Company	17,000,000	3	154,000	3	26,000	3721	BA
McDonnell Douglas Corp.	15,100,000	4	121,000	4	24,000	3721	MD
Rockwell Intl. Corp.	12,500,000	5	112,000	5	350	3721	ROK
Allied-Signal Inc.	11,900,000	6	110,000	6	1,600	3724	ALD
General Dynamics Corp.	9,550,000	7	103,000	7	200	3721	GD

*(Addresses have been omitted to save on space.)

What if you wanted to determine which companies had already gone through the inevitable layoffs of the 1990s? Compare the companies by the number of employees needed to generate a dollar of sales. Divide the sales by the number of employees. General Dynamics' sales per employee would be 9,500,000,000/103,000, or $92,233 in sales per employee. GE would be 50,100,000,000 divided by 298,000, or $168,120 in sales per employee. GE is selling more goods per employee, which isn't surprising considering the huge employee layoffs GE has undertaken.

More cuts could be on the way for other, fatter companies. Yet if you work for a company that has already made the cuts, the downside could be longer hours due to fewer hands; the upside could be more opportunity for growth due to increased responsibility. There's no perfect company. Each offers advantages and drawbacks, but a company that has already shed some fat may be a better bet for your future employment.

6. *The CEO's Background and Management Style*

The CEO sets the tone for the company. Is the CEO a domineering bully who has all his managers walking a tightrope or walking out? Or is the CEO a laid-back kind of boss who believes in decentralized management? What do the profiles in regional and national news magazines say about the CEO? The CEO has an impact on everything from the recruiter's lunch expense-account budget to his chances for promotion. Enough said. Know the CEO. Here's how:

Check *Who's Who in Commerce and Industry*. Note where the CEO went to school. Many companies prefer to recruit at schools attended by the CEO. Pull articles on the CEO from *Forbes* or *Fortune*. If it's a small company, check the local newspaper index or city business newspapers for articles on the boss. Even calling the local newspaper editor in the town where the firm is based may turn up useful information (if it's a small town). If the city paper has a business editor, ask him or her about the company. *Standard & Poor's Register of Corporations, Directors and Executives* will give you a few facts on the boss as well.

7. *What You Offer the Company. What Need Can You Fill?*

You must convince the company that it will make more money from your services than it spends on your salary. Too many job seekers focus on their own need and not the company's. They think, "I wish this company would hire me because I need a job." Instead, they must discover why the company needs them. After reviewing the skills inventory in Chapter 2, reviewing the job description, and ascertaining the company's strategy, you must ask: What does the company need? And why are you the best person to fill that need?

For example, if the company plans to expand in retail banking, it needs people willing to work in branch banks. If the company wants to open 200 new franchise shoe stores, its immediate need is for people with retail experience or retail potential. If you can point out how your skills (persuading, communicating, etc.) relate to the jobs in the areas it plans to expand, you have a much better shot at the job than the ignorant job seeker who comes in begging for work with no idea of what the company needs.

By the way, never assume you fully understand the company's needs. Your research merely prepares you to ask intelligent questions and to have answers ready that demonstrate how you potentially fit the company's strategy and needs.

8. Why You Want to Work for This Company

This means you've got to be able to articulate the difference between the company you are interviewing with and its competition. Unacceptable answers include: "I like working with people. I like big companies." These answers say nothing about the company. Acceptable answers include: "I've looked over the management policies of this firm and its rate of growth, and it seems very conservative; I tend to see myself as conservative, too. I think I would fit in well at the firm, and I'm excited about the prospects for growth."

Summary
Here is a summary of the steps to follow for researching large publicly held companies:

1. Look up the company's primary standard industrial code (SIC) in *The Million Dollar Directory* or *Disclosure* (on-line listing of 10,000 publicly held corporations)

2. Print out the company report from *Disclosure*, if available. Note competitors, market sold to, and earnings growth compared with industry.

3. Photocopy your company's primary industry section in the *Standard & Poor's Industry Survey* and the *U.S. Industrial Outlook*; also, copy the section on the industry that supplies your company and the industry your company sells to. This helps you see your industry's pressures.

4. Check *Infotrac, The Wall Street Journal Index, The New York Times Index,* and *Business Guide to Periodical Articles.* Print out a listing of article titles related to your company's business. Also, print out profiles on chief executives of your company. Look up the articles, copy, or take notes.

5. If you have a foreign-owned firm, *Foreign Manufacturers in the U.S.* will tell you the SIC code. Then use the first source listed above to research the industry in general. Specific company data will be hard to come by for foreign-owned firms or privately held firms. You can, however, understand the industry

well enough and study the competitors carefully. Some libraries have a European version of *Disclosure* you can use to check on European firms. The *Thomas Register of American Manufacturers Company Profiles* is another excellent source of basic information (number of employees, etc.) on foreign-owned firms. Check out a current book on the home country of your foreign-owned firm. Ask the reference librarian for books on cultural taboos in other cultures.

6. Check *Who's Who in Commerce and Industry* for information on the CEO.

Finally, before accepting any job, you must consider the following question: How will the job enhance your knowledge base? What will you learn in the job that you could sell elsewhere?

Make several copies of the following form and use it to gather information at the library.

COMPANY RESEARCH FORM

Position applying for: _____

Contact name & title: _____

Company name: _____

Address: _____

SIC: _____

Phone: (_____)_____ interview date: _____ thank-you note sent: _____

The company's best-selling products

Disclosure _____ Annual Report _____

_____

_____

_____

The industry (problems, opportunities, outlook)

January issues of *Forbes* and *Fortune* _____

U.S. Industrial Outlook _____ *S&P Industry Reports* _____

_____

_____

_____

The company's growth strategy (how will it make more money?)

Annual report _____ 10K _____ *The Wall Street Journal Index* _____

_____

_____

The company's financial condition (sales/revenues increasing?)

Annual report _____ *Moody's* _____ 10K_____

Value Line _____ *Disclosure* _____

(debt to equity, earnings, growth rate compared with industry, comparison of finished goods to sales/revenues, comparison of costs to sales) _____

_____

_____

_____

_____

The company's chief competitors and market position (how does the PE ratio compare with closest competitors?

Infotrac _____ 10K _____ *The Million Dollar Directory* _____

Thomas Register of American Manufacturers _____

State industrial directories_____

Is it on top? Check *The Million Dollar Directory* first for ranking (check *Thomas Register* for competitors of small firms). _____

_____

_____

_____

_____

The CEO, his or her background, and management style

Who's Who _____ profiles in *Forbes* _____ *Fortune* _____

BusinessWeek _____ local newspapers _____ *The Wall Street Journal Index* _____

Regional Magazines (such as *Georgia Trend, Crain's Chicago Business* and others) _____

_____

_____

_____

_____

What you offer the company. What need can you fill?

_____

_____

_____

Why do you want to work for this company? What sets it apart?

_____

_____

_____

_____

How will the job enhance your knowledge base? What will you learn in the job that you could sell elsewhere?

_____

_____

_____

_____

_____

_____

How to Research Small Companies, Nonprofit Organizations, and Government Agencies

Small Companies
Small but growing firms can offer real advantages. Generally, because there are fewer people, you have more responsibility from the outset. If you do well, your work may be recognized and rewarded. Often you can gain much broader experience in a small firm—experience you can sell to a larger firm later on. Or, you can stay on and grow with the company. On the other hand, small firms with no growth prospects may not be such a good move—unless your daddy owns the company.

If your prospective employer is small or privately owned, you can still track down the necessary information, though it's tougher to do than for big firms. Small firms are often not listed in the big directories, but your research strategy is the same as it is for large firms. You want to know the firm's financial stability, growth prospects, and how it stacks up against the competition.

Find answers to the following questions on small firms:

1. What's the product and who are the competitors? If it is a manufacturing firm, start with the *Thomas Register of American Manufacturers Company Profiles.* This book is like a national yellow pages where manufacturers advertise their products to other firms. Even tiny manufacturers advertise in it. It will give you an idea of what products the firm makes. Notice the other firms listed next to yours with similar products. They are the competition. Look them up in *Disclosure* or *CD Corporate,* the computer-based search programs available at large libraries. Or, check the sources listed in the previous chapter for information on the competition.

2. What industry does the company operate in? Even if you can't get information from any book on this specific small company, you can get a broad and essential look at the industry your company competes in from *U.S. Industrial Outlook* and *S&P Industry Reports.* Chances are good that the same problems that plague the rest of the industry plague your company—and the same growth opportunities. Dig in and get to know what drives the industry, who buys the products and what the outlook is.

If you can't get a copy of the annual report, look for every reference to the company in the *Thomas Register of American Manufacturers Company Profiles* and write down the products the company makes. Based on the products, determine the industry. For example, if the company makes machine tools, find the SIC number for the machine tool industry and look it up in the *U.S. Industrial Outlook* or *Standard & Poor's Industry Surveys.* Also check the January issue of *Fortune* magazine, and ask the librarian which issue of *BusinessWeek* profiles small and growing companies.

Trade associations can provide you with good contacts within the industry. Remember, what people know can give you an edge; ask about industry growth prospects and threats to that growth. Call the trade association and just chat with the association director. It's the association's job to represent the industry to the public and government. They'll talk. Ask.

Drive by the location of the firm, if it is nearby, and just look at it. Is the grass cut? Does it appear to be well-maintained?

Check *Inc.,* a business magazine, for general coverage, especially of smaller firms. Also, check local newspapers for company news and regional business magazines for current news.

The Small Business Administration (SBA) branch office in the town where the company does business will have general information on the climate for small business in your company's industry. The SBA will not provide confidential information on your firm, but it may provide useful information on the industry's prospects in the region. For example, the SBA may be able to tell you how many competitors your business has locally and projected population growth.

3. What are the annual sales and number of employees? Check state industrial directories. Ask the reference librarian where to find them. Often these directories will tell the address of the firm, the number of employees, and annual sales—information you won't find anywhere else. Once you know the annual sales, you can find the closest competitor in the *Thomas Register of American Manufacturers Company Profiles* and compare sales. Even tiny firms are listed in state industrial directories.

If you don't have access to a state industrial directory, call the Chamber of Commerce (during business hours) in the city where your company is based. It can tell you how many employees the firm has and how long the firm has been operating at that location. Obviously, the longer the firm has been in business, the better sign of stability to you as a prospective employee.

Call the Better Business Bureau to see if any complaints have been filed against the firm. A few complaints may not be reason for serious concern, but the Better Business Bureau may refer you to the state Bureau of Consumer Affairs. If the Bureau of Consumer Affairs is investigating the firm, consider it a red flag.

4. The CEO. Tougher to find, information on small-firm CEOs is still valuable. Check local newspapers for stories on the CEO. Note how long the CEO has been there and where he or she came from. If the CEO spent 20 years at another large firm and recently joined the organization, information about the previous company might be worth looking at, since the CEO's experience there is the source of his or her knowledge about management. If the CEO made his or her name as the person who built the former business's international division, international expertise may be the reason the CEO was hired for your firm. That could signal a move that the firm wants to develop international markets.

*Researching
Not-for-Profit
Organizations*

Should you accept a job with a hospital, university, social welfare organization, or community group? Here are a few pros and cons.

Yes, work for a small nonprofit if you are truly committed to the cause and if you like working in an environment where you receive little or no training and where you direct your own work. Working with others who share your beliefs and values can be fulfilling. Other benefits from working for nonprofits include greater job security than business jobs (if the organization has a stable income), impressive titles, and mobility to other nonprofit jobs. Jobs as directors, administrators, and fund-raisers require fewer steps up the ladder to attain in small organizations, though to increase your salary substantially, you must usually move to another institution. On the negative side, large and small nonprofits often lag industry in management issues. Few nonprofits invest in management training for their employees at the level and quality of private industry. As a result, nonprofits can be governed by the whims of poorly trained managers.

Large nonprofits differ from small lower-budget nonprofits in that the larger organizations often have many layers of management. Unlike private industry, which has downsized and cut layers to compete in the marketplace, large nonprofits supported by contributions or tax assistance have not been forced to make the cuts. Someone once said mediocre people rise to the top in nonprofit organizations, and in some cases this is true. The people who make the fewest enemies tend to be promoted. The jobs they are promoted to are often high-level administrative jobs. Because nonprofits often don't have to compete for customers and market share, they can afford to hire and promote people with good political skills and marginal talent. On the other hand, nonprofits that compete with the private sector are more likely to look for managers with vision and the ability to get things done. If you have the patience to work within the system, sometimes in a bureaucratic setting, you may enjoy nonprofit work.

Do not work for a nonprofit if you want to build a track record to move back to the business world, however. Businesses often do not know how to evaluate your work in a nonprofit organization unless the job has a comparable counterpart in industry, such as a systems analyst position. If the skill you use can be translated, you may be able to make a move back to the private sector. For example, writers in nonprofits can become journalists. Nurses can move to other nursing jobs. Human resource managers may be able to move to similar positions in business. But if the nonprofit doesn't have a counterpart in the private sector, don't take it unless you want to make nonprofit work your life's work.

As with regular businesses, you must determine how the organization makes money. Nothing lives on air, especially nonprofit organizations. Here are some issues to research before the interview:

1. Who is on the board of directors, and how long have the members served?   The richer the board, the more committed the board, the better. How much do board members give out of their own pockets? In a strong organization, board members contribute hefty sums every year because they are committed to the cause.

Check out the organization's annual report. Frequently contributors will be listed there by giving level and years of giving. Board members will be listed as well. Do the board members' names appear in the highest level of giving (often designated as a president's circle or patron's club)?

If the organization's offices are accessible to you before the interview, look for clues of giving, such as rooms or wings of the organization named after board members. If any of the board members are affiliated with private or public foundations, go to major libraries and look up the foundation's giving record to determine whether the foundation gives, and how much it gives, to your organization. Only large libraries with a foundation collection keep the microfiche cards listing foundations' giving records. Ask the foundation director of a local development office (at a university or hospital) which libraries have this information available.

If the board is primarily made up of social workers, schoolteachers, or clergy, the organization has not succeeded in attracting deep-pocketed supporters. You would certainly want to know the organization's plan for broadening and deepening the board's support and sphere of influence. (In other words, how are they going to attract the big guns?) The organization may still be worthwhile, but how much it grows depends on its sponsors and board members or other sources of consistent support, such as a strong annual fund-raising effort. Grants that are renewed every year are another good sign of stability.

2. What is the level of the person scheduled to interview you?   If you have questions about the financing and strategic plan that your interviewer cannot answer, and it is not the initial screening interview, think twice about the job.

You want to be interviewed by someone who is high enough up to answer the big questions about the organization.

3. What does United Way know about the organization?   If the organization participates in United Way fund drives, it must supply United Way with information. Talk with the local director of United Way about the organization's track record and the community's support for the organization.

The organization may not yet have an established track record. That shouldn't necessarily turn you off. For instance, many organizations have sprung up overnight in response to the AIDS crisis, supplying important and desperately needed services. These organizations may grow and give you a real sense of purpose. If the organization is new, ask about its long-range plans. Ask about how much of the organization's time is spent in delivering services, as opposed to administration. In the beginning, the best organizations spend most of their time actually dealing with the problem they came together for in the first place. You may become a key player and a valuable resource in a new and growing organization because it has not yet reached the bureaucracy level of large nonprofits. New organizations appreciate people who get things done—not mediocre paper shufflers.

4. How is the organization funded?   Ask the following questions after you get the job offer; you don't want to scare them off in the initial interviews. And by the time they make you an offer, your relationship with them will be close enough that they will be willing to share information with you.

- What percentage of funding comes from grants, contributions and fees?

- If the majority of the funding comes from contributions, how stable have they been over the past several years?

- Are the grants multi-year grants? Are they usually renewed?

- What services does the organization supply for fees? Who pays the fees?

- What is the trend in fees (growing/declining as a percentage of costs)?

- How long have they offered the service for a fee, and who else offers the service?

What you want to find out, in general, is how stable the organization's cash flows have been over the years. If the organization gets 95 percent of its money from a tax-supported program and 5 percent from contributions, you would want to know the organization's plan for increasing contributions.

If the organization receives 95 percent from contributions, and contributions have been stable over the years, what are the odds of increasing the contributions? With inflation increasing prices every year, contributions that remain stable represent a net loss that is compounded every year that contributions don't keep pace with or exceed the rate of inflation.

Organizations that depend on fee income generally must compete with other organizations for market share. If this is the case, find out the competitors and services offered. How competitive are your organization's services, and what is the perceived quality of the services in the community?

5. What is the organization's mission?   The mission is the organization's reason for being. It defines the essential services provided and reasons why the services are needed. How will the job you are hired to do relate to the mission? It would be comforting to think the people who carry out the organization's mission would be those rewarded most. Unfortunately, that is not always the case. In nonprofits, the people who make the most money are those who bring it in (fund-raisers, physicians, administrators). The good-hearted social worker fulfills the organization's mission but is rarely compensated for the good work he or she does. Therefore, your role in fulfilling the organization's mission may or may not create job stability and income growth.

First, ask whether the organization has a mission. Then look for evidence that shows that the mission is successfully carried out. The better the evidence of this, such as the number of people served and the existence of strategic plans for even better service delivery, the better the chance the organization has of attracting support for contributions, especially corporate and foundation grants. And, of course, the more prominent the board members are, the better the chances the organization will be successful in attracting support, because a prominent board will be better able to sell the organization's mission to potential donors.

Researching Government Jobs

Government jobs can offer job security and opportunities for promotion, as can jobs in the nonprofit sector. Also like the nonprofits, moving to the private sector from government jobs can be difficult because business employers have trouble comparing government work with private-sector work.

For some workers, however, government jobs' pluses outweigh the negatives. The government screens for skills and abilities and offers an equal chance of employment, unlike the private sector, which is still largely run by white males, despite the strides women and minorities have made in recent years. Government jobs offer career growth and tracking systems, and the pay is beginning to match pay in the private sector.

Government jobs offer one of the largest branching networks for growth in the world. As the world's largest employer, the U.S. government employs more than 2 million people worldwide. Even in the slow recessionary year of 1992, the government had 150,000 job openings.

Here's how to apply for jobs with the federal government.

Get the Federal Job Opportunities List. You can obtain this list from the Federal Office of Personnel Management by calling 912/757-3000. The list is updated on the 1st and 15th of every month, and 90 percent of government employees get their jobs by applying for jobs from the list. You can ask for lists that apply to the entire United States (called nationwide lists); your region of the country (regionwide); or a local list applying to your state (local list). The job list is also available on a computer bulletin board. If you have a modem, you can download the entire list or the portion that applies to the region of the country you wish to work in.

Apply. Ask for an application, called a SF 171. It comes in three pages. Tear along the perforated lines and photocopy it. Treat the application as you would a good resume. Use concrete examples of what you have done. For example, if you are applying for a job as a writer and you worked for the school newspaper, indicate how many articles you published. If you have specific experience in government accounting or a course or project in that area, say so if you want an accounting job.

Attach a photocopy of your transcript. The application offers only three lines for education; list only significant courses on the three lines. List co-op positions under job experience. Find a way to express your work experience positively, as you did on your resume. Demonstrate a skill or knowledge gained on each job you list, even if it's just getting along with people or using heavy equipment.

Don't limit your choices. If you provide a very narrow salary range or geographic area, your chances of getting a job are reduced. The government will keep your application on file for one year and match it to available positions.

Be sure to apply for the position before the position's closing date. The government keeps positions open for a limited time period; thus, it's especially important to stay up to date on the opportunities list. If you learn of a position and you don't think you have enough time to make an application, call the office at 912/757-3000. The application will be mailed within three days, and you can find out if you can still be considered.

If your grade point average is 3.45 or better on a 4.0 scale, or if you are in the top 10 percent of your graduating class, you can apply directly to a federal agency without completing the 171 form. You may apply to the Administrative Careers of America, which offers 112 occupations available to graduating scholars. Scholars who qualify do not have to take a written test and begin working at a higher wage scale. The government ranks employees with numbers and letters. For example, a GS5 is the grade or level of jobs that graduating seniors qualify for. A GS7 is the grade for persons with one year of work experience or a graduate degree. If you enter government service as a scholar, you enter at the GS7 level automatically.

Maneuvering Within the Government System

If you want to get into jobs with the Internal Revenue Service (IRS), Federal Bureau of Investigation (FBI), or other highly competitive areas, and your grades don't meet entrance requirements, consider taking a lower-grade position and moving up. According to a federal employment specialist, as many as one-third of IRS agents move up from clerical positions (GS4). You can even enter at a low level at one agency and transfer to another agency once you are in the system.

Temporary jobs offer another route of entry. The government defines temporary as up to four years, and 75 percent of temporary workers become permanent workers.

Here are some questions to consider about government positions.

1. Where did the last person in this job go? Outside the government agency or up a level? This gives you an idea of the mobility the job offers.

2. What is the turnover rate in the organization? If your predecessor and others in the organization are leaving in droves every year, something's wrong.

3. Does the government agency supply an essential service? For example, sewer and water services must always function, while social welfare positions may be at the mercy of legislators.

4. Is the agency funded by soft money or hard money? Soft money consists of grants and allocations limited to a specific time period. Hard money consists of line jobs within an organization that are permanent. Soft money positions may be eliminated if grants are not renewed. If the program has been funded for several years and is expected to be funded in the future, this is a good sign.

5. If the job is a soft-money job, what proportion of workers are hired on full-time in hard-money positions?

6. Is the job a merit-system job? Merit-system jobs, which are regulated by state law, often offer greater job security and greater opportunity for raises than non-merit-system government jobs. Jobs classified as merit-system jobs are evaluated by criteria set by the state, unlike non-merit-system jobs. Pay raises in merit-system jobs are often automatically keyed to inflation, while pay raises in non-merit-system jobs depend on how much tax revenue the state takes in each year. Merit jobs usually have a career track and thus more job stability, since they can not be arbitrarily cut in a low tax-revenue year. Ask what the typical career track is of the merit-system employee in the position.

7. How likely will budget-balancing laws in your state affect the security of the position? If tax revenue shrinks, will the government agency lay off workers?

Small Company Research Form

Sources checked: S&P ___ *U.S. Industrial Outlook* ___ Company 10K ___ Annual Report ___ Infotrac ___

State Industrial Directory _____ Local newspapers _____ *Thomas Register of American Manufacturers Company Profiles* _____

Position applying for: _____

Company name: _____   Contact name & title: _____

Address _____

_____

Phone: (   )   -   Interview date: _____   Thank-you note sent: _____

Business SIC Number & Primary Business (example; manufacturers and distributes fiber glass products, building materials, and piping products): _____

_____

_____

_____

_____

_____

Principal officers and recent management changes: _____

(Example: CEO graduated from Virginia Military Institute; came up through accounting ranks; has reputation for aggressive acquisitions; used to work at XYZ firm; articles report that he has cut back on perks, wants to move company to emphasize one or two product lines instead of 20; been with firm 20 years, due to retire. Source: *Who's Who, Fortune* article, 10K form)

_____

_____

_____

_____

Competitors: _____

_____

Industry position (what is its market share %?): _____

Geographic market area (where it does business): _____

_____

Strategy and current news (what's its big push right now?): _____

_____

_____

_____

Sales growth vs. finished goods inventory growth: _____

Overall strengths (e.g., management, leader in market, good financial position, good location, good training, stable company, growth opportunities, friendly coworkers) _____

_____

_____

_____

Overall weaknesses (e.g., high debt/low sales, possible takeover target, dead-end job, awful location, no training, no incentives for doing a better job, no career path, low salary) _____

_____

_____

_____

_____

_____

What do you offer the organization? What need can you fill? How will your job fit in with the organization's mission?

_____

_____

_____

How will the job enhance your knowledge base? What will you learn in the job that you could sell elsewhere?

_____

_____

_____

_____

_____

_____

_____

_____

_____

_____

_____

_____

_____

_____

_____

_____

_____

_____

_____

_____

_____

_____

_____

_____

Nonprofit Organization Research Form

Position applying for: _____

Contact name & title: _____

Organization name: _____

Address _____

Phone: (　　)　　-　　　　interview date: _____　　　thank-you note sent: _____

The industry (e.g., hospitals, universities, social welfare organizations: problems, opportunities, outlook)

Chronicle of Higher Education, industry newsletters (hospital industry magazines) _____

Infotrac (search for industry name, such as "social welfare organizations" or "higher education"): ___
Reader's Guide to Periodical Literature _____

(In general, will there be growth? Are there already too many hospitals serving the area? If it's a university, how does freshman enrollment look? Is it going up or down? How do these numbers compare to averages for hospitals or colleges? If it is a social service agency, who else provides the services offered? Will government grants be available to fund the services the organization provides?) _____

_____

_____

The organization's growth strategy/strategic plan (How will it better fulfill its mission, and how will it finance it? More contributions, grants?)

Annual report _____ Interviews _____

(What does it say its plan is?) _____

_____

_____

_____

_____

_____

The organization's financial condition (contributions, fees, grants)

Interviews _____ Annual reports _____ _____

(percentage of funds that are generated from fees, percentage from gifts, percentage from government sources and stability of each)

_____

_____

_____

_____

_____

_____

Organization's chief competitors and market position _____

(Example: a 500-bed hospital offering laser surgery and specialized oncology; no other hospitals in area offer these services) _____

_____

_____

_____

_____

The director, his or her background, and management style; the tenure and giving level of the board.

Who's Who _____ Annual report _____ Rooms named after board members _____

profiles in organization newsletters and local newspaper stories (see business pages and society pages, scan on microfiche) _____

(Example: director came up through organization; has a reputation for aggressively cutting costs, about to retire, likes golf. If your job is cost-cutting, you will be well positioned. If the director wants to put a new quality program in place, and you will be working in the quality area, you are also well positioned.)

_____

_____

_____

What can you offer the organization? What need can you fill? How will your job fit in with the organization's mission?

(Example: the mission is to provide health care; you will be managing insurance forms; job offers adequate authority to work with physicians and insurers to cut costs—or, job offers *inadequate* authority to make a difference in costs or service delivery.)

_____

_____

_____

_____

How will the job enhance your knowledge base? What will you learn in the job that you could sell elsewhere?

(Example: I will learn how to set up new programs in a bureaucratic organization and cut red tape to get things done. Or, I will not have adequate authority to make any real changes, but I will learn the computer system, and similar organizations will hire me if I have this knowledge. Don't take the job just to learn how to work with other people; you can do that at McDonald's. List at least five things you expect to learn that you could sell to another employer—obviously not trade secrets, just skills or useful knowledge.)

_____

_____

_____

_____

_____

_____

_____

_____

_____

_____

_____

_____

Screening Risk

The Brown Shoe Problem

It's no joke when you hear the odds are against you. Interviewers think they can spot the winners. Some may. But most simply pick people whom they perceive to be like themselves. One college recruiter told a story about an applicant who had an interview with the CEO of a major bank in the Southeast. The hapless applicant had worn brown shoes to the interview. Brown shoes! The recruiter was appalled. He and the other recruiters joked behind the applicant's back after he went in to the interview that maybe they should check the applicant's size and give him a pair of their black wing tips.

How silly can recruiters be? Very silly. This narrow-minded shoe-color thinking is what you need to know about to breeze past recruiters like the one mentioned above. Packaging is *very* important. And since applicants to this bank were expected to wear charcoal-colored suits and black shoes, the applicant had obviously not done his homework. Never mind that the applicant may have been brilliant. Recruiters, at least poorly trained ones, look at packages.

The same recruiter told me he thought students were basically all alike. He said he just looks for the ones who look the best and talk the most fluently. Good companies hire better recruiters, ones who can actually spot talent and aren't overly impressed by packaging. But since you can't predict what the recruiter will be looking for, play it safe. Your goal is to get around the recruiter and get inside the company for an interview.

Interviewers look for applicants who look neat and well-groomed. Clean, well-tailored, pressed clothes, neatly styled hair, and shined shoes are musts.

Dress   Read John Molloy's *Dress for Success* if you are unsure about appropriate dress. The following tips are basic.

For men:
- Wear a suit, not a sports coat.

- Wear black shoes, not brown; shined.

- Wear a starched white shirt; check the collar to make sure it's not frayed.

- Wear a dark, understated suit; never polyester, never shiny (be sure the collar doesn't stand out from your neck in the back).

- Wear socks that come up high enough not to show your shins.

- No jewelry.

- Shirt cuffs should show at your sleeves (an inch, no more).

- Wear a tan raincoat, if needed.

- Get a haircut, and shave off your beard or mustache for conservative employers.

Be sure to have two suits, one for the screening interview and one for the selection interview. Both should be conservative, grey, navy, or charcoal wool blend or other blend. Neither should be all polyester or seersucker cotton. If unsure, go to a good men's clothing store and have the suit tailored to fit you.

For women:

- Wear conservative shoes (pumps, no sling backs).

- Wear a quality dress or suit.

- Wear a blouse that harmonizes with your coloring (consider silk or a cotton blend; avoid evening fabrics such as shiny satin).

- Wear small, expensive jewelry (no excessive gold chains).

- Your hair should be shoulder-length or shorter, professionally cut.

- Your makeup should be understated, but do wear some. No cologne.

- Nothing sexy—no bare skin, no skirts that ride up.

Again, quality is the rule. Linen suits are elegant but wrinkle as soon as you sit down, so avoid them for interviews unless they are blended with a material that is wrinkle-resistant. Look for good-quality wools, rayons, and wool blends. Be sure your suit jacket is lined. Put an extra pair of panty hose in your briefcase. If you are not wearing a jacket, consider using dress shields to prevent perspiration stains under your arms. Remember, polyester makes you sweat no matter what the temperature. Cotton blends are best in humid climates. You may want to avoid a purse altogether and just carry an extra copy of your resume in a briefcase or small folder. Office supply stores carry small leather folders for about $20.

As a rule buy a quality, expensive suit and avoid fashionable or flashy clothes unless you are interviewing for an advertising or creative position where the style is more relaxed. If money's a problem, charge it. Your interviewing clothes represent an investment in your future. If you are serious about getting a job and interview with enough companies, you will get a job. Then you can pay off your clothing investment with your first six month's pay. This investment is not frivolous. If you try to go on the cheap, you may never get in the door.

Dress is so important that one recruiter advised students to sit in the parking lot of the company and observe how the executives were dressed before choosing clothes for the interview. If you know the person who is going to interview you and see the interviewer on another occasion prior to the interview, note what colors the person wore and the style of jewelry, if any. If you are a woman, try to pick an outfit in the same color range. Psychologists say this immediately promotes harmony between people. It helps people feel psychically tuned in to each other. This "tuning in" process is often unconscious.

Remember, the more recruiters perceive that you are similar to them, the more they will like you.

Bargain hunters may want to try second-hand shops close to good neighborhoods for clothing. The castoffs of the very rich may fit beautifully and have originally cost many times over what you can afford to spend. For $200, you may find a classic suit or dress that originally cost $800. If you try it on and love it, it's worth the money.

On the day of the interview, avoid drinking coffee (the caffeine may be overstimulating and make your hands shake) and avoid smoking (the smell will send an ugly message). Do something to relax: go for a walk, jog, work out, drink herbal tea, or practice closing your eyes, breathing deeply, and visualizing yourself as confident and friendly. See the interviewer smiling at you and offering you the job or recommending you for a second interview.

Visualization implants the positive outcome in your mind. Once you see the positive outcome, you move in that direction with enormous confidence. Conversely, if you spend time telling yourself you don't have a chance and no one will ever hire you, you will propel yourself to that outcome.

The Body Language Trap

Interviewers are looking for clues about you—not just from what you say, but from the way you sit, move, and look at them. They think they can determine whether you are deceiving them by analyzing your body language. According to human resource consultants, the powerful candidate is relaxed and leans forward toward the interviewer. (We are not concerned here about whether these notions have any scientific validity; what we care about is playing a game to win.)

So, how are you going to send the right message? Get control of your body language. You are on stage from the moment you walk into the company waiting room or campus placement center and sit down. As writer H. Anthony Medley points out in his interviewing manual, *Sweaty Palms*, the interviewer may well make up his or her mind about you in the first 4 minutes or the first 30 seconds. If you make a bad impression at the outset, you have a tougher job in changing the interviewer's mind. While still in the waiting room, sit up straight, leaning forward, almost on the edge of your chair, to convey aliveness and enthusiasm. If you tend to cross your leg and shake your foot when you are nervous, don't. Women should avoid crossing their feet at the ankles and tucking their feet under the chair, since this conveys submissiveness. Obviously, don't smoke or chew gum. Rest your hands on your knees or hold a handkerchief to absorb the perspiration on your hands. Sweaty palms make clammy handshakes.

While you are waiting for the interviewer, breathe deeply. There's a special way to do this. As you inhale, make sure that you breathe from your stomach. If you are not sure you are doing it correctly, place your hand on your belly; as you inhale, your hand should rise. Now hold that breath for a count of 10 and exhale, pushing out the last of the breath. You won't believe how relaxing this is. You feel like a whole load has been dropped from your shoulders.

Bring a copy of your resume to the interview. When your interviewer calls you in, rise, shake hands firmly, make eye contact, smile, and walk into the office. In a good handshake, the palms touch, and the muscles are relaxed enough to allow full contact between palms. Don't give the interviewer a weak or fishy handshake. Never hand someone your fingers to shake. And don't give women wimpy handshakes. Shake everyone's hand in the same way: full palm contact, wrist parallel with body and not twisted to the side. Give two firm shakes, maybe three. Smile. Wait to be asked to sit down.

Keeping your back straight in the chair, lean forward toward the interviewer. Don't get too comfortable; rather, strive for an alive and alert look. When students practice this posture in videotaped interviewing, they immediately recognize how effective this alert posture is and how sloppy or distant other postures look.

The interviewer may be looking for body language signals that he or she thinks indicate your truthfulness, credibility, etc. Personnel specialists seem to think they can catch you in a lie if you tap your toe or tap your fingers on the table nervously. Common sense might tell them that nervous gestures are just a sign of nervousness, not deceit. But since recruiters are buying into this nonsense, let's beat them at this game. Don't shift around in your chair. If you are given a swivel chair, don't let yourself swivel around. One recruiter told me the company deliberately uses swivel chairs to catch nervous applicants who swivel. Apparently, the company has a two-way mirror in the room to observe the applicant. So, don't swivel, even if you are by yourself. Keep your hands and feet relaxed. No toe tapping or wringing of hands. Keep your hands away from your jewelry, hair, and face; let them stay relaxed in your lap.

Don't cross your arms or lean back in the chair. Lean forward, maintain a steady gaze but not a staring contest, smile frequently, paraphrase what the interviewer says, and listen carefully.

In general, applicants who smile, make eye contact, and convey high energy get more offers than applicants who remain stony-faced or look down, according to one study. An impression of low energy or overly controlled or frozen behavior makes a poor impression. The screening interview is superficial, so much so that poor body language can get you thrown out.

What to Say

The cold hard facts are that interviewing rarely identifies the best applicant. Recruiters often make hasty decisions about candidates with biased information. They rate applicants on impressions rather than facts. Many recruiters use unstructured interviews, which means they have no real plan and no systematic way to compare answers across candidates. The questions interviewers ask may not have been thoughtfully related to the actual job tasks or behaviors needed on the job.

Interviewers tend to have their own theories about what makes people tick, and they devise questions to elicit information confirming those theories. They may ask how clean you keep your car because they think clean cars are a proxy for some other behavior; the question may have no relevance to your job performance. Unless they have tested the question scientifically and related it to a specific job behavior, the answers are meaningless. But don't tell interviewers that. Many interviewers are convinced they can get a grip on your total personality, motivations, and work habits through an interview.

No matter how silly an interview question seems, you must remain poised and friendly. Answer all of their questions to the best of your ability. Your goal is to put them at ease with you. Put yourself in their shoes. They are trying their best to find the right person. Make it easy for them to choose you by being well prepared and receptive to their questions.

Your first interview will probably be with a screening interviewer, or screener, who does not have the power to hire you. Screeners are trained interviewers who verify that you meet the basic requirements for the job. Screeners often select applicants who they feel will fit in or "look good" back at the home office. They look carefully at how you dress, how you present yourself and how similar you seem to the people who already have jobs in the department they are hiring for.

Screeners look for people who won't pose problems for the company. Never say you can't do something until you've failed at it. Never say you didn't like your previous boss. Stay positive, enthusiastic, and upbeat when talking with screeners. But don't talk too much. Just tell a few well-rehearsed, natural sounding stories that you identified in Chapter 2. Communicate confidence, poise, and friendliness. For entry-level positions, screeners are looking for people who are willing to be trained, who look the part, and who won't be problem employees.

To interview successfully, you must be able to communicate who you are to the interviewer in 20 minutes or less. And you need to make him or her biased toward you, in some way. For example, if interviewers perceive you as "warm," they also perceive you as generous, good natured, happy, sociable, and wise, according to human resource experts McGovern and Tinsley. If they see you as cold, they will lump you with the unhappy, irritable, and humorless crowd. To look warm, smile sincerely and make eye contact. Be as friendly as you would be meeting a relative or an old friend. Consciously put yourself in that state of mind, that the interviewer is an old friend or someone you like very well. This might be criticized as acting, but it's really projecting warmth while still being yourself.

If for some reason the interviewer doesn't break the ice, break it yourself. Weather conversation is always safe. In the South, small talk is king, and people talk weather aggressively. For example, if it's a Friday and the sun is shining, you could say, "Gee, it's going to be a great weekend for hiking," or fishing or waterskiing. You are testing the water here. The interviewer, anxious to be done working and to get into the weekend, may brighten up and ask where you hike.

An event or situation common to both strangers usually supplies good conversational openers. Big-city people in the North like to talk traffic and commuting times. Sports can be a good icebreaker if a major event such as the World Series is being played by a local team. Otherwise, sports doesn't always work. If you happen to be interviewing in the screener's personal office, avoid making conversation about photographs of children or spouses. When students come into my office and comment on the pictures of my children, I find it difficult to switch gears, and it doesn't really break the ice. But if they come in and notice on the wall my class listings and the enrollments of the classes I work with, I can talk easily about my job as a communication consultant. It's a professional question rather than a personal one, which makes me more comfortable.

Be prepared to answer why you want to work for this specific company. The company wants to feel you are really interested in it. For example, you wouldn't tell a woman you want to marry her because she is a woman, right? You want to marry her because she is special in particular ways. Well, companies are no different. Don't tell a company you want to work for it because it is a big company or it has a good training program. Presumably, many other companies are also big and have good training programs. So what sets this company apart? The recruiter wants to know. And if you did your homework, you will know.

A Typical Unstructured Screening Interview

Trained interviewers follow a pattern of questioning they hope will (1) relax you enough to talk, (2) probe your resume and experience for problems, (3) sell you on the company, and (4) provide you with an opportunity to ask questions.

During the screening interview, answer only the questions asked. Don't volunteer information, but don't limit yourself to yes or no answers. You want to show that you can talk articulately about yourself. Be prepared to back up what you say about yourself with examples and stories. Interviewers tend to remember stories; they tune out canned answers. For example, tell them about the time you organized the sorority's social event. How did you approach it, and what was the result? Be sure to get to the point right away. If the interviewer doesn't feel he or she really knows you, the interviewer may not risk sending you to the home office for a second interview. Knowing your product—that's *you*—is crucial to communicating effectively during an interview. Knowing the company is the other important step.

The unstructured screening interview will probably begin with an icebreaker.

The Icebreaker

Interviewer: Good morning. Did you have any trouble finding us?

The interviewer isn't asking this to determine whether you are bright enough to read a map. Truly, it is to relax you. By talking about directions and street signs, you tend to forget your nervousness about being interviewed. If it is a campus interview, the interviewer may have already searched your resume for something that he or she has in common with you. The interviewer may say that he, too, was a member of your fraternity or that he had once travelled through your home town. The interviewer wants to get you talking and acting as natural as possible so that he or she can get to know the real you.

Probing Questions

Interviewer: "I see from your resume that you had six part-time jobs in 12 months; could you tell me a little about that?"

The recruiter wants to know if you will stick with the company if you come on board. Look over your resume for problem areas such as a string of six jobs in 12 months. Be sure you have a true story with a positive ending ready. Here's an example of a reasonable answer to the interviewer's question:

> *Applicant:* "That's right. If I were you, I would probably wonder about that, too, so let me tell you the reason for all the job changes that year. My parents were in the process of a messy divorce. In retrospect, I must admit that it hit me pretty hard. Since that time, I've sorted out the issues and have now held my current job for a year. And I think that if you contact my current employer, he will give you an excellent reference on my work."

You've resolved the recruiter's doubt. Be sure to be honest when dealing with sticky issues, and always point out how you have resolved the problem. Read on for more ways to handle probing questions.

"What do you want to be doing in five years?"   Make sure your answer is honest, but not unrealistic. You could say that what you are going to be doing in five years depends on the typical career track for someone in this position. Or, since you already know what you like doing (from the skills list in Chapter 2) you could say, "I'd like to be doing [whatever it is you like] in a way that provides [whatever reward is important to you—financial, independence, creativity, flexibility, authority, etc.]." There is no right answer to this question. The only wrong answers are options that wouldn't be within the realm of the company. For example, if you just want to get training to go on to another job at another company, this obviously is not a good answer. You don't want even to hint that you are planning to leave. And, of course, you don't want to say you plan to be the CEO of the company either—at least not right away. Let's be real.

"Tell me about yourself."   This is a tough one. The best way to handle it is to have prepared a brief discussion of your academic record, outside activities, or personal interests. Ask the interviewer which area he or she would like to hear about. That way you know that you are addressing the right question. Without this preparation, job applicants tend to wander; and for some reason, they always begin with, "I was born in Waukegan, Illinois," and then ramble through a hodgepodge of high school and who knows what else. Meanwhile, the interviewer is fighting off yawns. So be prepared to ask what the interviewer wants to know.

"What salary do you expect?"   Don't bring up money until the interviewer does. When the question is asked, don't answer right away. Ask what the range is for the position. If you feel your qualifications exceed the stated job requirements, ask for the top of the range. You won't get it, but ask. Be sure to justify why you are worth that much in terms of the *company's* needs, not yours. They frankly don't care that you have a car to pay off. If you are entry-level, ask for a salary in the middle range and don't be surprised if it's at the bottom of the range. The company needs enough leverage to move you up with merit increases. Ask about merit increases and what standards are used to evaluate performance. This information could be crucial to your future happiness.

The Sales Pitch Now the interviewer tells you what a wonderful company it is and how the opportunities are unlimited. Please, don't over-rely on what the recruiter says about the company. In a survey I conducted of graduating seniors, 69 percent said the recruiter's confidence in the company influenced them "very much" in deciding to accept an offer. The interviewer, at least at the college-recruiting level, is a salesman.

Listen carefully to the recruiter's pitch. How does the interviewer back up his or her claims? Does he provide evidence? For example, if the recruiter says there is unlimited growth, ask about the career track of others who have been hired into this position. How long did it take them to get there? Ask about the rising stars in the company. Are they all men? You may want to think twice if you are a woman or minority in a company that is governed by the "good old boy" mentality. Is the recruiter specific about what work you will be doing and how it will be evaluated? What was his or her career track with the company? If the recruiter were to change something about the company to make it better, what would it be? Does he or she really know what kind of person works best in the position?

Your Questions Maintain eye contact with the interviewer while speaking and listening. Use your stories of achievement when describing your skills. Ask what a typical day on the job is like. Ask how your performance will be evaluated. Ask about training provided, choices of work locations, the typical career track for this position, merit increases, and benefits.

Notice that this interview does not probe for skills related to the job you will actually perform. The interviewer asks about your career plans, presumably to determine whether you are goal-oriented. Whether being goal-oriented actually relates to the job is subject to question. The probing question is a valid attempt to find out whether or not you will stick with the job.

Closing The recruiter will probably say he or she has several other people to see and that he or she will get back to you. Express your excitement about the job and tell the recruiter that you really want the job (if you do). If it is a sales job, consider asking the recruiter to make a commitment to you right then and there. Say, "I'm really interested in this job and ready to start work. Can we move ahead on this now and set up a starting date?" This brash move can be effective in sales positions, and it may work for other positions as well.

Finally, be enthusiastic, smile, talk about things you know and are comfortable talking about—success stories, stories about what you like to do, how you've approached projects. You will look more alive and relaxed when you talk about something you know well. Not all interviewers will ask the questions that let you show your best and most relaxed self. It's up to you to select the topics that make you the most comfortable. If you have researched yourself and the company, you will appear poised and confident. Be sure to *get the interviewer's business card, in order to have the proper address for a thank-you letter.*

For now, remember these screening interview tips:

1. Shake the interviewer's hand firmly.

2. Smile warmly.

3. Make eye contact.

4. Try to find something you like about the interviewer and focus on how much you like the interviewer.

5. Say nothing negative—about your former boss, school, anything. Stay upbeat, positive, and enthusiastic—that's the rule.

6. Project relaxation, confidence, and friendliness.

7. Be prepared to tell the interviewer why you want to work for the company. Phrase it in such a way that it is clear to the interviewer that you can tell the difference between his or her company and its competitors. Look back at the research chapters in this book. If you haven't done the research, you are not ready for the interview.

8. Dress professionally.

9. Follow up with a thank-you note within 24 hours.

If you are interviewing with several people at an office visit, slip into the restroom and jot down notes after talking with each interviewer; that way you will have specific information that relates to that person when you write your thank-you notes. Generally, however, you will have only one screening interview.

Coping with the
Structured Interview

More advanced companies are beginning to use structured interviews to screen applicants. Unlike the unstructured interview I've just described, structured interviews are designed to compare applicants' responses to a set list of questions that relate to the skills needed for the job. Questions such as, "Can you give me an example of how you handled a deadline?" are typical of structured interviews.

The questions are designed to identify how you might react in real-life job situations and how you have handled tough situations in the past. The structured interview is also used to eliminate interviewer bias, which may result in candidates selected just on looks or vague impressions. Your answers will often be tape recorded and compared with other applicants' answers. Since employers are using structured interviews more and more, you need to be prepared to answer the tough questions they pose.

The following questions are intended as a trigger, a reminder about events in your life. There are no formula answers to these questions. Interviewers have heard all the formula answers, anyway. Be honest, be positive. If you struggled with something, show how you have come back and are dealing with it now.

Jot down your answers to these questions. The last thing you want is to be stumped when an interviewer asks a tough question. Think your answers through carefully. You will find that you have more to offer than you realize.

Typical Structured
Interview Questions to
Rehearse

Work often involves completing jobs within a defined time limit. Some jobs have flexible deadlines; others have pressure deadlines. Knowing how you handle this can be important when you are evaluating several job opportunities. Many business jobs involve a team effort, though some jobs have a more independent focus. Which do you prefer? If you can tell an interviewer a story about how you handled these situations, you will impress the interviewer and have a better chance at getting the job.

Think back to a time when you had a deadline. How did you handle it? What was the result? How do you feel about deadlines?

_____

_____

_____

_____

_____

Think back to a time when you were working with a group and something went wrong. What did you do to make things work again?

_____

_____

_____

_____

Tell me about a situation in which you were responsible for establishing a course of action for yourself and for others to accomplish a goal. How did you go about planning assignments of people to jobs?

_____

_____

_____

_____

_____

What was the result?[1]

_____

_____

_____

_____

_____

1. I wrote these questions as possible behavior dimensions that are frequently measured in assessment centers. The dimensions include: planning and organizing, delegation, control, decisiveness, initiative, tolerance for stress, adaptability, and tenacity. The dimensions were identified by George Thorton III and William Byham in *Assessment Centers and Managerial Performance* (New York: Academic Press, 1982).

People make decisions in a variety of ways. Tell me how you feel about allowing subordinates to make decisions. Can you give me an example of how you have made decisions with a group? What was the result?

_____

_____

_____

_____

_____

In large organizations a certain amount of control must be maintained. Can you tell me about a time when you had to establish procedures and monitor the progress of people working under you? What did you do? How did you follow up to make sure the work was done? How did the people working with you react to your following up? How did you feel about their reaction?

_____

_____

_____

_____

_____

Sometimes everyone has trouble making decisions. Tell me about a difficult decision you have had to make in your life. How did you approach it? What was the result?

_____

_____

_____

_____

_____

Tell me about something you are committed to. How did you become committed to it? What actions have you had to take to become and to remain committed?

_____

_____

_____

_____

_____

If you had to choose between (1) a class assignment that offered thorough directions and a sample to follow or (2) a class assignment with few directions and no example to follow, which would you choose? Assume that the grading of the first assignment relied on following the sample exactly. Would you enjoy that kind of assignment? Assume that the second assignment offered no directions but could potentially count for more of your grade. Which of the two assignments would be more comfortable to you?

_____

_____

_____

_____

_____

Sometimes supervisors offer little direction. Can you tell me about a job that you did with little direction or supervision?

_____

_____

_____

_____

_____

Many people find change difficult. Can you tell me about what things you did to make the transition from high school to college? What helped you most? How were your grades during your first quarter (semester)? Can you tell me about the times you have had to adapt to a new job or a change in environment? What did you do to make it easier for yourself?

_____

_____

_____

_____

_____

Tell me about a time when you had to stick with a goal. It may have been a diet, a study program, or maybe even a plan to save cash for a ski trip. How did you go about sticking with the goal? What were the obstacles? How did you overcome them?

_____

_____

_____

_____

_____

Jobs that require employees to deal with the public can be stressful. Can you describe an example of your experiences in dealing with the public, especially hostile customers? How did you handle difficult customers?

_____

_____

_____

_____

_____

A Little Trap to Avoid

You know those pesky application forms? Well, more than one applicant has been disqualified for not filling them out neatly and carefully. But you say, "I'm an important person; they can look at my resume." Sorry. They will look at your resume, but if you are too self-important to fill out the application carefully, your resume will get tossed in the trash can. That's reality, folks.

The Company Interview

How Can You Tell If the Job Is in the War Zone?

You made it past the screening interview. Congratulations. You know how to dress, smile, act trainable, use body language, research companies, and, of course, you have the basic qualifications for the job. The second interview is the selection interview or company interview. You will be talking with people who have the power to hire you. But they don't hold all the cards. You will also be able to evaluate them and decide whether the job will bring you fulfillment or combat duty. Jobs in war-zone offices are far too common and far too stressful.

The selection interview differs from the screening interview in several ways. First, selection interviewers are rarely trained in interviewing. After all, a selection interviewer is simply the person you will ultimately be working for. Often selection interviewers don't ask you any questions, or at least not questions that allow you to show yourself off. They may ramble on about the company or the position. They may base their hiring decision on the most ridiculous factors. In sum, they are human begins who make mistakes. Selection interviewers often don't hire people every day, and they may not even know how to plan for an interview.

It's your responsibility to identify what they want and then sell yourself using your stories and examples. At the same time, you want to scope out the environment to determine whether you would be happy working there.

Since you and all the other candidates have the proper credentials (or you wouldn't be there), the hiring decision depends on one simple idea. *Do they like you?* When all is said and done, the person who gets hired is the person whom everyone likes the most.

So how do you get people to like you? Simple, act like you really like them. It doesn't hurt to really like them, by the way. Think about the first time you realized you liked someone who is now your friend. Before you developed these positive feelings for the other person, the other person probably expressed an interest in and liking for you. You felt okay when you were around that person, and we all need to feel okay. Communicate that same liking for your potential employer if you want to be hired.

Adjusting Your Style to Fit In: Understanding Their Communication Styles

Another way to get them to like you is to communicate with them in a manner that is comfortable for them. Salespeople have to deal with this situation every day, and you can learn a great deal about how to approach the selection interview by examining how good salespeople quickly tune in to their customers to make the sale.

In his excellent sales textbook, *Personal Selling: An Interactive Approach,* Ronald Marks suggests psyching out the customer (interviewer) so that your approach effectively meets the customer's (interviewer's) information needs.

Marks says good salespeople know that there are at least four different personality types, and each expects to be approached in a different way. If you don't know this basic information, you may not hit it off with the prospective employer. The four types are: Drivers, Analyticals, Expressives, and Amiables. Though most people are a mixture of different personality traits, people often rely on one style more than others. Identifying the dominant style will help you be more sensitive to your interviewer's information needs.

Drivers   Drivers, for example, are the stereotypical hard-driving executives. They are impatient, get-to-the-point people. A Driver once interviewed me for a job and announced at the beginning of the interview that he had ten minutes. He looked me straight in the eye and said, "Tell me about yourself." I stammered around for a few minutes looking for the right approach. I said I was looking for a job that would be fulfilling and that I could be committed to. Obviously irritated by what he thought was sentimental drivel, he shot back, "What makes you think this job will offer you that?" My anger rising slighting, I coolly responded, "That's why I'm here; to find out." He liked that, but my minutes on the firing line were not over.

"We are gearing up for long days as this operation gets into full swing," he warned. He mentioned 18-hour days. I told him that maybe the job was not for me since I have children, and my husband already worked those long hours. I told him I believe children need at least one parent at home. In fact, I had decided that the job was not right for me. Yet months later, when another position opened, I found this same driving interviewer was trying to recruit me to work for the company because I had been honest, and I didn't flinch in the face of his aggressive interviewing style. Sometimes Drivers enjoy give and take; if they push, push back, but don't try to dominate them. Be businesslike and professional and don't waste their time.

While my approach to this interview turned out fine, you want to be sure you have a Driver before you respond in an equally aggressive way. Look around the office for clues. A Driver generally has a power-office setting. He or she is behind the desk and you are on the other side of the desk. Drivers have awards and achievements on the wall. They may have several stacks of paper on their desk, and you get the feeling they know what's in each one of them. They may appear rude. They are poor listeners and don't want to be bothered with details. They are bottom-line people. Talk results with them and achievements, and for heaven's sake, don't tell them your life story. They may seem cold and efficient. They will be impressed with you if you cut to the chase and show them how you can improve the department to make them look good.

Amiables   Not all interviewers are Drivers, however. You may be interviewed by an Amiable. Amiables have squeaky-clean offices with pictures of the kids and artwork on the walls.

They are great listeners and want to be called by their first names. They will decide whether they like you based on the personal relationship they develop with you. They like to chat. You may find yourself making small talk and laughing and never getting to the hard stuff of the interview. Play along with them. This is how they evaluate people.

Amiables are also fussy about details. Be sure you look sharp and have an error-free resume. They go crazy when small details are wrong. An Amiable will look more carefully at the quality of paper you use and the effectiveness of the presentation than the content. But heaven forbid they find a typo.

Amiables are also very concerned about protecting their staffs. Often they will want to consult other staff members on their opinions before taking action. Consensus is the way they rule. Be patient and show that you get along well with people by using stories that emphasize working well with teams. Amiables are also indecisive. You may wait a while for them to make up their minds while they consult everyone on their opinion of you.

Analyticals

Analyticals are even more detail-oriented than Amiables. They usually have charts and graphs on the wall and have a functionally decorated office—usually all in brown. Analyticals don't even seem to notice color, and rarely display artwork. Be patient with them as they pick apart every detail of your resume. Back up what you say with facts. Be logical. In fact, if you say things like "if you look at it logically" or "it stands to reason," you will impress them. Ask them questions about how they go about solving problems, or, better yet, what their approach is to analyzing problems. Ask about the company's quality program and ask them to describe which approach the company uses to analyze processes and correct them.

When pressed for one of your stories of achievement, talk about how you analyzed a problem and solved it. Emphasize the steps you take. Try to think in a logical, linear way. That means build a discussion the way you would build a logic problem: if x is true, then y is true. That way you will be on their same wavelength. Offer to send them more information about yourself at the end of the interview if there are still questions. Don't push for a decision. Acknowledge as you are leaving that you know they will want to analyze all of their candidates to make the best choice.

Expressives   If you are interviewed by an Expressive, be prepared for a warm, enthusiastic greeting. Expressives often have cluttered offices decorated boldly, or in the latest style. They are impressed by status symbols and feelings. If you worked for IBM or another Fortune 500 company as a student intern, they will be impressed. They make decisions based on intuition and their "gut feelings." Talk feelings with them. Ask an Expressive to give you the company's "big picture." Ask where he or she *feels* the company is going. Don't bore an Expressive with details; Expressives prefer drama and flash, and, above all, status. Provide solid evidence of what you have done in school or on the job, but don't go through each step you took to get to the result, as you would for an Analytical. Get to the point with Expressives.

You don't have to change the way you are; you simply need to stay tuned to the needs of your prospective boss. If you walk into the office of an impatient Driver and waste his or her time with chitchat, you won't get the job. On the other hand, if you walk into the office of an Amiable and push for a decision or act too businesslike, you won't get the job.

Interviewing can be like a detective game. As you walk into the office of a Driver, you look around and watch him or her carefully. Listen for cues. If you find it is a Driver you are talking to, get to the point and ask the tough questions. If it's an Amicable, chitchat. Analyticals want details, and Expressives want to hear your "gut" feelings on the job. You can practice discussing your experience in different ways with a friend through role-playing.

How to Approach Different Personality Types
NON-RESPONSIVE

ANALTYICAL

- Stick to specifics.
- Don't overstate what you can do.
- List advantages and disadvantages of all alternative plans.
- Put things in writing.
- Provide solid factual evidence for what you say.
- Do not rush the decision process.

DRIVER

- Keep relationship businesslike.
- Stick more to "what questions"; avoid "why questions."
- Do not waste time; make your points as quickly as possible.
- Be efficient and discipline time.
- Be precise.
- Provide alternative actions with their probabilities of success for achieving his or her objectives.

NON-ASSERTIVE ———————————————— **ASSERTIVE**

AMIABLE

- "Actively" listen.
- Move along in an informal way.
- Be agreeable.
- Discuss personal opinions and feelings rather than facts and logic.
- Provide personal assurance that the actions you are suggesting involve minimum risk.

EXPRESSIVE

- Don't hurry the discussion.
- Don't argue; look for alternative solutions.
- Be entertaining and fast moving.
- Always specify and solidify detail.
- Use testimonials and special incentives.
- Show that you are interested in him or her as a person.

RESPONSIVE

SOURCE: Reprinted with permission from *California Real Estate,* copyright 1992 by the California Association of REALTORS®, all rights reserved.

In the selection interview, be sensitive to the interviewer. If he or she is all business, don't crack jokes. If he or she wants to talk about sailing, talk about sailing. Be sure, however, to bring the discussion back to focus on you and the job.

Ask the interviewer to describe the ideal candidate. Then explain, modestly, how your qualifications and skills meet the criteria using stories of achievement.

Of course, don't raise the money issue yourself. Let the interviewer bring it up. Keep the interviewer talking and answering your questions. Have a give-and-take conversation. Be sensitive to the interviewer's body language. If things are not going well, ask for a cup of coffee to get things back on track. Often a break can give you time to collect your thoughts and think of questions to refocus the interview back in your favor.

Ask what problems they see and what opportunities are available within the company. Use your research on the company and ask about the company's strategy. Listen carefully. Selection interviewers will unwittingly tell you a lot about the company and its politics. Interview him or her and consider whether you would like working with this person. Be relaxed and likeable. Smile and project that you really like the person without being phony. Focus on what you like about the person. Even if you feel tempted to judge the interviewer in a negative way, don't.

Stress Interviews

By subjecting you to a very stressful interview, companies attempt to see how you will handle pressure and difficult situations. In a stress interview, you may be berated ridiculed and insulted by prospective employers. While most companies are moving away from this interviewing technique, a few may still subject you to this test.

For example, they may ask why you attended such a rotten college. They will poke around for the right button to push to set you off. One student, faced with the insults of the stress interview, walked out of the interview. Needless to say, he didn't get the job.

Stress interviewers want to see how you cope with pressure. Don't let them get to you. Stay calm, no matter what insults they hurl at you. Answer their questions with as much dignity as you can muster.

Consider calling them at this game and ask why they would want to make someone feel uncomfortable in a job interview. This gives you more sense of control over the situation and turns the tables on them. Then they have to justify their inappropriate behavior. But if you do call them, do so with a spirit of geniality and friendliness. Smile. Let them know that you know that they are essentially better human beings than their behavior indicates.

Some interviewers may ask you to sell them a pack of gum or a pencil during an interview. This, however, is a legitimate test of your selling skills, not a stress technique. Do your best to sell the gum. Here are some tips.

1. Ask the interviewer about his personal needs: How would he like to use gum? Does he smoke? What

qualities make various gums attractive? Flavor, color, long-lasting qualities?

2. Point out how this gum meets the interviewer's needs.

3. Ask the interviewer to answer "yes" questions: Does he agree that chewing gum relaxes him? Does he agree that spearmint gum freshens his breath?

4. Would a price of 25 cents fit into his daily budget?

5. Offer to sell him the gum for 25 cents.

6. If he objects that he can't afford the gum or raises some other objection, overcome this objection with a good reason.

7. Close the sale.

When interviewing for a sales job, always ask for the job during the interview. The recruiter wants to know that you would have enough confidence to ask for the order in a real sales situation. Recruiters have been telling me that they wish more applicants would ask for the job in every case. Be bold, but be friendly. Go ahead and ask for the job if you think the interviewer is a Driver or an Expressive. Soft peddle with Amiables and Analyticals.

Listen to What the Company Says About Itself, But Take It with a Grain of Salt

During the selection interview, people will tell you what a wonderful company it is. You may be inclined to agree based on your company research. Don't accept surface information at face value. The following example shows why that can be dangerous.

A recent issue of *The Wall Street Journal* carried an expose by Susan Faludi on what it's really like to work for the privately owned Nordstrom Department Store chain on the West Coast. Listen to what the company says about itself:

> Nordstrom insists the system works. It says that employees get one of the highest base pay rates in the industry—as much as $10 an hour—and especially industrious employees can make as much as $80,000 a year. The company also says it only promotes from within and under its corporate policy of decentralization, managers have unusual freedom to make decisions.

Patty Bemis, a former employee who was recruited to work at the prestigious department store chain from her position as the Estee Lauder counter manager at another store, said, "We'd all heard Nordstrom was the place to work. They told me how I would double my wages. They painted a great picture and I fell right into it."

The reality was not a great picture after all. She and several other employees recently went public, describing a cutthroat enterprise where employees were asked to give their all for the store.

"The managers were these little tin gods, always grilling you about your sales," she recalls. "You felt like your job was constantly in jeopardy. They'd write you up for anything, being sick, the way you dressed. . . . In the end, really serving the customer, being an All-Star, meant nothing; if you had low sales per hour, you were forced out."

Faludi said other employees offered horror stories about Nordstrom's. They said they worked seven-day work weeks with no overtime. Clerks were expected to spend several hours stocking the inventory after they punched out in the evening. Relentless Saturday morning meetings were held to boost sales. The meetings were required but clerks were not paid for them. Employees who occasionally got sick were thought to lack dedication and put on the list to be scrutinized for dismissal.

If you looked at the financial information, you would see that Nordstrom had a soaring stock price and among the highest sales per square foot in the industry. Does that mean it's a good place to work? No.

So how do you find out whether a company is a good place to be? You ask tough questions in the interview. You call the Better Business Bureau and the state labor relations board. Find out if complaints have been filed against the business.

At the interview, ask yourself whether the people are friendly. Do they seem happy in their jobs and confident in the company? In a recent survey of University of Georgia business majors, I found 71 percent of our graduates said the perceived "happiness" of the employees significantly influenced their decisions to accept a job offer.

The Power of Atmosphere

People make the environment. If the people you work with share some of your values, or even understand you a little bit, you can overcome all kinds of other obstacles. You don't have to be best friends with your coworkers, but working with pleasant people who aren't continuously at war affects the quality of your work life. If, however, the atmosphere is cutthroat, think about how you usually do in competitive situations. How do you cope with conflict? When you have a fight with a girlfriend or boyfriend, what do you do? Do you withdraw, go for the jugular, pout, reason? How do you feel about conflict? The way you deal with conflict and competition in your personal life will probably be the way you deal with it at work.

Avoiding the War Zone

If you have ever worked in a war zone, you know the signs:

- Bosses compete for power, which means the rules change every day.

- Gossip is rampant. You are afraid to talk to anyone for fear of backstabbing.

- You must document everything you do for fear of being unfairly blamed or for fear that someone will steal your ideas.

- There are frequent closed-door sessions in which employees plot strategies

A company undergoing change may exhibit some of these tendencies. Change means a shift in the power structure. One way to look for signs of war-zone offices is to ask to see an organizational chart that shows the lines of authority. Then frankly ask how well it works. If there have been recent management changes, how well are they working?

Ask employees how they like their work. Ask them how it compares to other places they have worked. *Watch their eyes.* Do they look afraid to tell you anything? That's a clue. If they really like their jobs, there shouldn't be any fear. Watch for how uptight people are, how carefully they skirt your questions. Does everyone say that there are a few bugs to work out but they are confident that it will work smoothly soon? That's a bad sign, unless they can be specific about why things should work out.

The higher the position, the less the employees will tell you. Listen for signs of system-wide problems. If one employee has a problem with a supervisor, that's not worth worrying about. But if employees consistently can't do the work they were hired to do because of the management of the organization, think hard before deciding to work there. Look around the office. Does it look like a place you would like to be? Look for clues. In one interview with what seemed like a stuffy, formal company, I spotted the copying room on the way into the interview. A life-size poster of Elvis hung over the copy machine, and I knew the company wasn't as stuffy as it looked.

Ask about two-way communication. How responsive is management to ideas from its employees? Ask for examples if you can do so without sounding too aggressive. Companies that listen to employees are certainly preferable to those that don't. They lie about this, of course. Try asking a middle-level manager about the flow of two-way communication. But be specific. Ask when was the last time top management adopted an idea from lower levels. Ask what the process for two-way communication is.

You may wonder why two-way communication is so important. I spent a couple of years analyzing bank management performance reports for the savings and loan industry. Employees who worked for savings and loan associations that relied on employees for ideas also had happier employees. The associations with good two-way communication also tended to have a strategic plan that was the operating plan for the institution. Institutions that had developed a strategic plan but didn't follow it (or "stuck it in a drawer," as one disgruntled employee put it) had unhappy employees. Many poorly managed savings and loan associations failed. Middle managers know the true story of how well the organization is managed. Try to find out by using these indirect means, such asking about two-way communication and how closely the organization follows its strategic plan.

Eliminating Loser Jobs

The worst jobs pay little and extract much. They create heavy stress and offer little career growth. They are the jobs you went to college to avoid doing.

My rule for evaluating jobs is this: the less interested you are in the job, the more money you should receive to do it. If the job is a high-stress, low-paying job but is only temporary, you may put up with the unpleasantness if the price is right. But take the job only if you are starving and have to pay the rent or if you can gain a skill to sell elsewhere.

Look for a few road signs that will direct you to work that is compatible with your personality. Positive signs may include good bosses, having enough authority to match your responsibility, good hours, good pay, possibility of promotion or marketability of the skills you gain. Look back over the rewards you said you wanted out of a job. Are they components of the job you are considering?

Eliminating loser jobs also involves eliminating jobs with the "can't stands." Think about the following "can't stands." Which apply to you? Plan to find out subtly whether these negatives are part of the job. Obviously, you should never tell an employer that you can't stand anything. This is just for your private information—another way to eliminate the loser jobs.

Identify what you absolutely can't stand.

"I can't stand it when a boss is breathing down my neck." Or "I like knowing the rules and following them to the letter." Don't get a boss who wants to supervise you closely. Ask your potential boss how closely he or she wants to monitor your work. Ask what would be comfortable for him or her. Be specific: daily checking? signing off on all memos? Ask about training, procedures and how valuable attention to procedure is to pay raises and promotions.

"I can't stand it when I can't change the schedule or routine of my days." Or "I prefer a predictable routine." Ask people doing the job to describe a typical day. Then ask if that routine must be followed every day. What are the deadlines? If they are monthly, you may have more flexibility. If they are daily, you may need to stick with the routine.

"I can't stand it when there is no plan for what we are supposed to do." Or "I like to develop my own plans." Ask who sets policy. How is policy communicated? How closely do employees/managers follow the company's strategic plan? How free-form is the job?

"I can't stand it when I have to work with numbers." Or "I like the concreteness of working with numbers." Again, even non-number jobs may require some accounting. Get a clear description of all aspects of the job.

"I can't stand a lot of planning." Or "I feel comfortable setting goals and meeting them." Even if it's not a planning job, you may have a big share in developing a budget. Ask about the role of planning/budgeting in the job.

"I can't stand wearing a suit and tie." Or "I like a more formal business setting." Look around. What they are wearing is what you will be wearing.

"I can't stand working closely with other people." Or **"I really like having a lot of people around me to work with."** Ask how work is performed. How do the employees' functions interrelate? Is socializing required or routine? Look over the environment at the selection interview. Ask the employees how often they socialize. Ask about team projects.

"I can't stand being polite to obnoxious people." Or **"There are always a few difficult people, but in general I really like dealing with a variety of people."** Don't get a job in which you need to work with the public every day.

"I can't stand having to punch in." Or **"I like to keep regular hours."** If you habitually arrive late for work or dally a bit over lunch, some bosses will understand; others won't. If you go to lunch on the day of the interview, observe how relaxed the other employees are about their schedules. If you arrive for a morning interview when the office opens, observe when people come in. Do they look over their shoulders or check their watches?

"I really need more than two weeks of vacation." Or **"It wouldn't bother me to gradually work up to three or four weeks of vacation."** Consider working for the government or a nonprofit organization that is more flexible on vacation time. These jobs may pay less but offer more vacation days. State employees at universities in Georgia and South Carolina, for example, can start with as much as three weeks of vacation, plus a week at Christmas. Jobs in elementary and secondary education can offer summers off, but don't be fooled by the idea of lazy summers. Increased educational requirements for teachers force teachers to take postgraduate education courses every summer to earn more pay. Check promotion schedules carefully before committing to jobs in education.

The following questions need to be answered, but not all need to be asked in an interview, since some may prove uncomfortable for the interviewer. Ask to see a copy of the employee handbook that governs these issues. Inquire gently about the career path of predecessors. If none of your predecessors stayed with the company, it's not a really good sign, but not necessarily a bad omen, either.

1. Does the company offer both cost-of-living and merit raises to employees?

2. What achievements earn merit increases in your area?

3. What is the career track, the next step?

4. Is it possible to see a performance evaluation tool?

5. What is the job description?

6. Where is the position on the organizational chart?

How to Spot Potentially Bad Bosses

Working for bad bosses can be a major career downturn that depresses you and robs you of your creative energy and confidence. Deciding which bosses are bad bosses is a highly personal decision. Some are obviously bad—the tyrant; the woman chaser; the micromanager who checks your every detail and reams you out daily; the young, insecure boss who throws her weight around; the disorganized, always-in-a-tizzy boss; the back stabber; the abusive boss. You may have had some of these already.

The odd thing about bosses is that the boss you love may be the one others despise. The way you feel about a boss may have a good deal to do with how you felt about your family when you were growing up. Some people like bosses who ignore them and never praise anything they do. That would probably bother some people, but it feels pretty comfortable to them. If you had a controlling or smothering mother, you may go crazy with a boss who tries to be your mother. The similarity between a boss and an unpleasant experience you had as a child can unleash emotions that seem to come from nowhere, and you may not even realize that it is not the job but unresolved feelings about your parents that are intruding into the work place.

What many of us do, whether we want to admit it or not, is recreate our families in our work places. We assign roles to all the players. An authoritarian boss stands in for an authoritarian father figure. A conniving secretary becomes a jealous sister. Conspiracies with other employees against the boss are conspiracies against mom and dad.

Avoid this by thinking about the role you played in your family. How did family members treat you.? Were you the young prince who could do no wrong? Were you the one who took after your mother's side of the family and therefore not appreciated by your father's side? Chances are, you will drag this role into your job and do whatever you can to get treated the way you were treated at home—not because it was all that great at home, but because it is known and comfortable. So, if you were the prince, you will act the role of the prince—but watch out if you have a boss who grew up hating her princely brother.

Listen to yourself and to your feelings when you interview for the job. Do you have a sudden negative flash upon meeting the people at the prospective job? All you may have is the feeling and not realize it is connected to old feelings. You can do a couple of things to deal with these feelings. First, listen to the intuition that says avoid this place. Second, if you do take the job despite the negative vibes, see a psychotherapist to work through the negative reaction.

You don't have to be sick or problem-ridden to see a psychotherapist. The healthiest people are those who have seen psychotherapists at some time in their lives. They have the most insight, and they don't drag as much emotional baggage into the office.

If you can't afford a professional, do some thinking about your family. By now, you probably have an inkling about what drove you crazy about your mom and dad. What you might not know is how you developed behavior to cope with them. Look back over what you've written in this workbook about what is important to you and what you do well. Try to picture yourself changing your behavior to cope with mom and dad. What did you do to feel good about yourself in your family? What did you do to get your parents' attention (temper tantrums, high achievement, wrecking cars)? Do you still do some of these things to get attention at work? What role did you play? Once you know, you have a better chance of succeeding in your work, even if you get a boss who's the spitting image of your dad.

Therefore, when evaluating potential jobs, take a hard look at your potential boss. Does he or she do anything during the interview that flashes a little doubt through your mind? Listen to that doubt.

A woman I know interviewed with a female boss who began the interview with a sweet smile, but when my friend asked some probing policy questions, the boss's eyes went hard; she practically pounded the desk. Since my friend was from the North and was interviewing in the South, she assumed this potential boss was just struggling with reconciling her tea-party Southern manners with managerial aggressiveness. While that may have been true, the boss's split personality appeared and reappeared in the ensuing months of my friend's employment there. Temper tantrums, swearing at employees, gossiping about her own employees, and general brow-beating emanated from this Southern woman. She insisted on reading every memo that went out of the office. Six managers quit within one year. The boss still doesn't think she had anything to do with it.

Some bosses belittle employees, jump to conclusions, and fail to provide fair and honest performance reviews. How do you spot them? Ask probing questions. What do they like and dislike in an employee? Who is their hero or whom do they look up to most and why? What criteria do they use to evaluate their employees' performance in these positions? What kind of performance would warrant a promotion? Who has been promoted recently and on what basis? These are the difficult questions. If they can't answer them, think twice about the job.

While you are at the interview, ask the boss what bothers him or her the most. If the boss is upset because people come in a few minutes late and not because the sales are down, that tells you a lot about that boss. My opinion is that micromanagers like this are best for employees who enjoy routine and structure.

Your first job won't have everything you want. Your first job is your chance to demonstrate what you can do. Your goal is to do whatever your employers ask you to do, and much more than they ask. At the end of your first or second year, you want to have a sterling recommendation to take to your next job. Your goal in these interviews is to get your foot in the door and get an offer.

Write a thank-you note after every interview. Make sure you get the interviewer's business card for the address. Make the letter friendly and review the highlights of the interview. Restate your qualifications and your interest in the position. Mail within 24 hours of the interview. Send a note to *everyone* who interviewed you. Thank-you notes are typed using the same format outlined for cover letters.

Oh, By the Way, You'll Have to Take a Few Tests...

You are far down the track now. The company's managers have invested time and money in you. They've screened you; they like you. But there's just one more thing—the assessment center. Assessment centers test skills, traits, and abilities through a variety of paper-and-pencil tests and actual group interaction exercises. The company wants to find out how well you might do on the job using objective data. Tests may include aptitude tests, achievement tests (to determine what level of skills you already have), personality tests, intelligence tests, and work sample tests, which give you a real task to do that is similar to the one you will do on the job.

Before you freeze up or lose sleep over this, remember— they like you or you wouldn't be at the assessment center

at all. They really want their good evaluation of you con-
firmed. And you will do just that if you follow the tips in
this chapter.

Assessment centers measure your abilities using tests.
Tests have right and wrong answers. They also use inventories, which have no right or wrong answers.

In-Basket Tests   These real-life simulations require you to sit at a desk and
go through an in-basket of memos and activities that need
to be performed. You will be asked to sort through the bas-
ket and make decisions, rating the tasks in priority and performing some of the tasks. They will usually throw you a
curve, such as asking you to show up for your new employee
photo at 9 A.M., at the same time that you are to meet with
the boss to set the day's agenda. You may also be asked to
write a letter or perform an analysis in a short period of
time. Set priorities intelligently. See the boss, call and ask
to reschedule the photo, write the letter. Obviously, meeting
with the boss is more important than showing up for a photo
session, but it's important to be courteous to those who set
up the administrative functions as well.

Leaderless Group   You are in a group with other potential employees in this
Discussion   exercise. Your group will have a problem to solve. The assessors will watch to see how you interact with the group.
Take control of the situation by asking someone to take
notes (don't take notes yourself) and suggest in what order
each of the group members should speak. Look at your
watch to show you can plan, and don't let one person dominate the discussion. Be sensitive. After everyone has spo-
ken, ask each group member to list the strengths and
weakness of his or her proposal. When the assessors call
that five minutes is left, ask the group for its consensus on
the solution reached. So you see, the actual answer is less
important than the way you conduct yourself in the exercise. (By the way, the above advice comes from Brian Page,
whose excellent book, *Getting Ready for That Assessment
Center,* provided much of the material cited here. He has
studied how to achieve in the assessment center process.)

Role-Playing   You may be asked to role-play serving an angry customer
to demonstrate your interpersonal skills. The byword here
is to stay calm. Use empathic listening. If the person says,

"I think this whole business is rotten," deal with the underlying feeling: "Tell me how I can help. . . . It can be frustrating dealing with a bureaucracy." Empathic listening is helping the other person feel heard and understood without arguing or challenging the person, which would only make him or her more angry.

Handwriting Analysis (Graphology)

This is not used extensively in U.S. companies, though handwriting analysis is used extensively in Europe. Since I analyze handwriting and have taken more than 60 hours of course work in this area, I believe it reveals a great deal about personality. Yet because it has not been standardized, different analysts may interpret the same writing differently or may not take into account that handwriting changes from day to day, even from hour to hour. Traits in this afternoon's sample may differ a great deal from traits observed tomorrow. A good graphologist sees the whole picture and should collect several samples.

What will the analyst see? Everything from your sexual attitudes to your organizational ability. A good analyst should focus only on the traits and behaviors that have been identified as job related. For example, organizational ability is seen in the small letter "f." Discretion is in the closed and tied loops of the letter "o."

Despite my interest and belief in this study, I advise you to print carefully and to avoid handwriting for a job if a sample of your handwriting is requested. You are simply putting yourself at risk by allowing an analyst to evaluate you. The analyst may not have adequate training to observe the keys to your work habits. By printing, all you convey is that you tend to be an independent person who follows a different drummer. Printing cannot be read and is the safest alternative.

General Aptitude Tests

Composed of twelve separate tests, these timed tests together form an aptitude score. The tests measure intelligence, verbal aptitude, numerical aptitude, spatial aptitude, and analytical and cognitive skills. These tests will ask you more questions than you can possibly answer. Listen to the instructor on how the test will be scored. Keep track of your time. Take off your watch and set it on the desk. Fill in as many answers as you can. When time is running out, depending on how the test will be scored, fill in the rest of the answers, even if you don't know the answers.

Intelligence tests are used more and more for predicting how well you will do on the job. Research shows that they measure problem-solving skills and abilities that relate to job requirements in an increasingly sophisticated work place. There is no way to prepare for these other than to be well rested and do your best.

Fact-Finding Exercises

You may be given a paragraph describing a situation. Your objective is to ask questions of a resource person and identify as many facts as possible to come to a conclusion. Stay calm and ask as many questions as possible to isolate as many individual facts, and don't assume the resource person is part of the situation. The resource person is only a person able to supply facts. The more facts you identify, the better you will do on this test, according to Brian Page.

Personality Inventories

Not all tests measure job-related skills. Personality tests including ink-blot tests and tests that ask you to interpret ambiguous pictures are widely used to inventory your personality traits. Experts disagree on whether the assessment center personnel who score these tests have adequate experience or expertise to score these tests properly.

Many personality inventories were originally developed to identify people with personality disorders. Personnel specialists have tried to link the traits identified (as many as 18,000, from friendliness to analytical ability) to job performance. Yet there is little empirical support for this. About all the research in this area indicates is that people who are identified as kind and helpful on the tests may do well in a service or public contact job.

Self-report questionnaires, such as the Minnesota Multiphasic Personality Inventory, were originally developed for classifying mental patients by their degree of abnormality. Many assessment centers use this test to decide whether you will be a good manager, even though the test has no validity for predicting job performance.

Though these inventories serve to protect people from taking responsibility for their employment decisions, you can't fight or argue about taking these tests without appearing obstinate. There is no good way to advise you on filling out inventories other than to be honest. There are no right or wrong answers. If you can see a pattern that will allow you to project diligence and ability to set priorities, do it. Just stay cool. You'll be okay. Remember, they want you.

Waiting—You're Almost There

Waiting for a downtown bus to go to the library, you look down at your watch and suddenly realize you missed the bus. You know there will always be another, so you wait awhile longer. Finally you change your mind and flag the crosstown bus to visit your sister, skipping the library entirely.

What just happened here? You originally planned to go to the library but you ended up at your sister's. How often does the same thing happen in your job search? While waiting for the right offer, you suddenly shift gears. Maybe you thought you would live in Chicago and work downtown, but that job didn't come through. A better offer came from Des Moines and you took it. Or your fiancé got an offer in Detroit, and you decide to tag along because no offers have come through from Chicago.

We have such a strong impulse to want to control our future, especially if we tend to plan ahead, that the wait-

195

ing can drive us crazy or seemingly force us to change our plans. We start to believe that no other buses will ever come. But others will come; other options will surface. Waiting is something older people know how to do better than younger people. Older people know there's always another bus. For the next 20 years, the buses will come fast and furious. Some you will catch; some you will pass up. You may change your plans dozens of times and go in directions you never anticipated.

But while you're standing on the street corner, what's going through your mind is not that there are dozens of buses, but that if you don't catch this particular bus, your entire future is ruined. How often have you heard people say: "But if I don't marry this guy, I'll never get another offer," or "But if I don't take this job, I'll have to go back home and live with my parents." These look like simple either-or decisions: either A happens or B happens. But what ever happened to multiple choice? No, you don't have to marry the guy because you will never get another offer. Marry him because you want to be with him. If one person finds you attractive, ten other people will as well. The hard part comes in the waiting. You may not find Mr. or Ms. Right next week or next month, but you will find that person.

And by the same token, don't take the job because no other offers have come through yet. Bide your time; plant some more seeds; do some more interviews; take out a loan to support yourself so that you don't have to go back home. Remember the movie *Field of Dreams?* When the spirit world promised Kevin Costner that if he built the baseball field, the players of old would come and play, the players didn't show up right away. People doubted Kevin Costner's sanity; he doubted himself. But he waited. He planted seeds for the future, and he waited.

The Pleasure of Waiting

Understanding the value of waiting will help you enjoy life. Your life doesn't suddenly start when you graduate from college, or get a job, or get married. A new phase starts, but you were living all along.

Conjure up in your mind a picture of what you want. It may not come tomorrow or next year, or even in ten years, but it is there and you will find a way to make it real. What you are doing is beginning to shape your future using the right side of your brain. That's the creative, intuitive side. The left side will want to make lists, set goals, and make five-year plans. The right side wants only to see the picture. To begin taking charge of your life and your career, set goals only for today and use your mind to picture whatever you want in the future. Meanwhile, work, get a job, and what you want or something even better will come at you.

Waiting effectively means living today, planting seeds, getting your one goal for the day done and not worrying about tomorrow. The job you so desperately want may not come through, though a better one may when you aren't paying attention. Sometimes the seemingly inconsequential ideas that pop into your mind become the seeds of your future. If you suddenly see an article in a newspaper announcing a lecture on archaeology or some other topic that is not part of your career plan, but you have a feeling that it might be interesting, then go. The little "maybe" ideas often lead you to new information that for some reason helps you clarify problems or decisions that are in the forefront of your thinking. If someone suddenly asks you to do something out of the ordinary and a very small voice in your mind says "Yes," do it. Learning to tune into the very small voice called intuition can help you stay in the flow of your own positive direction. The rest of the world may not understand why you suddenly are taking acting lessons when you trained to be a nurse, but, after all, the rest of the world is not living your life. By paying attention to what you are doing today, you build a structure that allows you to get what you want in the future.

So taking initiative in your job search starts with seeing a piece of the happy future as clearly as you can. The future resists planning; it happens. The way to let it happen positively is to find a way to become very good at several different things or very, very good at one thing. That is your job security—your skill or skills.

Detours: The Marriage Option

How do people approach the waiting period before the offers come through? Very differently. Those who absolutely must work in downtown Chicago will overlook offers from other places. They will hold out for the right offer, and if they are patient, they may get just what they want. Those who stay flexible or who are less patient will be more likely to consider a wide range of options and may accept offers for reasons that have little to do with their still fuzzy career goals.

For example, while you are waiting for a job offer, you

may decide to marry. In fact, you may decide to marry *because* no good job offers have come through. Then the best-laid plans go awry. Often exceptionally bright young women (and a few men) have come into my office to say they must get a job in Valdosta, Georgia, or Cedar Rapids, Iowa, because that is where their fiancé is working. It makes me wonder if the fiancé *is* the career.

Why has this sacrifice been so freely made? Will that bright young banking student be sentenced to limited career growth in these small- to medium-sized cities? Sometimes the towns are even smaller, and the only jobs available are those that wouldn't require college in the first place. There are a few things wrong with this strategy.

The cold, hard fact that one in two marriages fails must be reckoned with. You have only a fifty-fifty chance that you will still be married to this person seven to ten years down the road. You must get a good enough job to support yourself on your own. If you want to have kids later on, then perhaps one of you can stay home. But if no children are involved yet, make sure you live in a big enough town to allow each of you adequate career growth.

I'm not down on marriage at all. In fact, I married while I was still an undergraduate and have gotten along fine for the past 20 years of marriage. I'm not saying that you must wait. But do think about both of your careers. Neither of you should have to suffer.

What to Do Now That You Have the Job

11

At Last—An Offer!   You have an offer, maybe more than one. Congratulations! But how do you decide which job is best? And how do you hold them off to wait for the one you really want?

Relax, don't rush. Truly, you have all the time in the world. When the first offer comes in, you may wish to wait for something better. Ask the first caller what the acceptance deadline is. If the company wants to know tomorrow, do you really want to work for that employer? Recruiters have been known to offer an extra $500 for accepting right away. Who needs a high-pressure salesman when you are making a decision that will affect you for one to two years? Don't be intimidated by high pressure. Ask if you can get back to him or her within a reasonable period of time (perhaps two weeks or a month).

Which job is best? That really depends on you. What is the most important aspect of a job to you? If money is the biggest issue, go for the job that pays the most; if location is important, pick the desirable location. Which company is the most stable? Which offers you the rewards you identified in Chapter 2?

Should you negotiate for more money? Sure. But keep in mind that you don't want your new employer to see you as a problem employee. Most jobs have salary ranges. If you are an entry-level applicant, they generally will offer you salary at the bottom of the range. Ask what the range is. Also, negotiate other aspects of the job, including hours, company benefits, or whatever is important to you. See Herb Cohen's *You Can Negotiate Anything* for the best advice on negotiating. In a nutshell, don't push. Be friendly, be patient, and take your time. Don't antagonize your potential employer and start off on the wrong foot.

How to Succeed on the Job
Evaluate Your Boss's Needs

Build a good relationship with your boss. The boss determines whether you get a raise, promotion, or dismissal. Your first assignment is to ask him or her about priorities. Don't assume you know what's important. Ask. Then make sure that you always do *that* work first. Never keep your boss wondering whether you will meet a deadline. Do it ahead of deadline and let the boss know when the job has been completed. Provide progress reports on longer jobs. Finish everything the boss gives you and come back asking for more. Be cheerful and loyal and do your best to build a good relationship. Now is the time to show initiative. You may not get any direction at all; the boss may just point to a desk and say go to work. Plunge in and do the job and check with the boss on how he or she would like to be kept informed of your progress.

After you've done what your boss says is most important, let him or her know you did it. Let other people know it, too. Career strategist Adele Scheele suggests sending memos out to the important people in the company if you come up with a really brilliant idea so that you will get credit. Then tend to the other aspects of the job.

Observe the Achievements That Get Promotions or Raises

In staff meetings, who is getting praise and for what? Who is listened to and who gets cut off? The people who are taken seriously have power, even if they don't have a high position, and they usually have information that is useful to the organization.

Who is getting promoted? Sometimes the stated goals

are not the actual goals of an organization. You may think you are doing the job right "by the book," but maybe the boss doesn't run the operation by the book. That doesn't mean you should run your operation in an illegal or unethical way to please the boss. If the boss is unethical, leave and find another boss. But first be sure you know what the norms of the business are. As in any new situation, sit back and listen and observe before jumping in with both feet. Get to know the players. Who generally seems to have the best information about what is going on? Listen to what the best-informed employees say. Observe the personal style of the top executive of the firm. What kinds of people does the top executive surround herself or himself with?

Remember what we said about selection interviewing and personality types? That still applies. Be sensitive to the information needs of the boss. If the boss is a Driver, get to the point, talk bottom line, and point out how your idea will make the boss look good. If the boss is an Amiable, chitchat and check your details; if an Analytical, offer to supply more data for decisions and don't rush decisions; if an Expressive, talk gut feelings and sell your ideas with status symbols and drama.

Evaluate Your Boss's Boss's Needs

Let's pretend for a moment that your boss is mentally out to lunch, and the rest of the department knows it. Should you figure out what your boss's boss wants and ignore your immediate boss? That's a tough one. My advice is never to go around your boss to the next level. If you can work and somehow get recognition for what you do despite working for an incompetent boss, do so. Otherwise leave or ask for a transfer. But don't rat on your boss; it just doesn't lie right.

Build Trust

If your boss doesn't trust you to do anything on your own, either he or she doesn't trust anyone or he or she just needs more experience with you to let things go. Ask the boss for small assignments first, follow up on details, write up a report or memo documenting what you did, and keep a copy. Ask the boss to go over the work with you to ascertain what the boss is looking for and how the work could be improved. You want to build a good relationship with your boss so that you get a sterling performance review after one year.

Avoid Being a Rude Upstart

When you are in a new situation, don't stomp around the office trying to change everything in the first week. It's a surefire way to make enemies. Instead, wait, watch, and listen. Get a feeling for the rhythm of the office and the power centers.

If you have been charged with changing things in the office or plant, and some folks just won't go along with the changes, don't feel you are a failure. Do your best to meet their needs by listening carefully to what they say. Paraphrase their objections to be sure you fully understand them and to be sure that they feel understood. (That may be half the battle.) Do your best to negotiate changes that they will find acceptable by attempting to meet their needs. And above all, don't take it personally if they don't want to do what you suggest.

If they still don't want to do things your way, you may have to go ahead and implement the changes if your boss has told you to do so. Be firm, consistent, reasonable, and friendly.

Tell people about changes face to face, and also use a friendly memo. Remember that anger, hostility, and personal feelings have no place in memos that can haunt you after the anger has passed.

Learn the Business

You may not be in the position to achieve much during the first year if all you do is keep your head down and do what everybody asks you to do. To achieve in the first year, you need to spend every spare minute learning the business. If you are in the credit department at a large retail chain, for example, don't just learn about credit; learn about how the chain makes money, what part of the chain makes the most money, and how. Read company reports, but also read *The Wall Street Journal* and *The New York Times*. Look for articles that relate to your company and industry. Join a trade association and find out how other credit departments manage their accounts.

Treat Subordinates with Respect

Secretaries are human beings with feelings and dignity. Never ask a secretary to perform anything but typing, filing, and the other work that is judged on a performance review. Secretaries and administrative assistants are not your personal slaves. No errands, no coffee, no pampering. You are not helpless.

Treat subordinates like human beings. That means *asking* them to do things, not telling them. It means being sensitive to their time constraints. Get your work done in advance so that you don't create a crisis for secretaries or other staff members. We have a sign in our office that says, "Failure to plan on your part does not constitute a crisis on my part." And that's just what we tell students, faculty, or anyone else who try to dump their self-created problems on other people at the last minute.

It's tough to be on the bottom rung of the ladder, but don't take it out on your underlings. Ultimately, you are judged in life not by the successes you rack up, but by the kindness you show. Besides, bullies get little peer respect and often cause problems that the bosses end up solving. You will just look foolish if you bully your staff. You may even create a turnover problem, since good people rarely stay in jobs supervised by bullies.

The funny thing about jobs is that to advance, you sometimes have to change your entire job. If you are an engineer and want to make more money, you may have to become a manager of engineers, or a newspaper reporter may have to become an editor. These are fundamentally different jobs. You stop being a reporter when you start being an editor. Though editors make more money, there is no reason to try to advance to that level unless the skills required are your best skills (supervising, editing, negotiating, setting up). A good company should offer you some reward for doing a job well without forcing you to grow out of the job into something entirely new.

But if it doesn't, develop solid skills in what you do and search for projects with quantifiable results to maintain your marketability and security. Will someone on the outside pay you for what you know how to do? And can you prove what you can do by presenting an achievement portfolio—a list of projects you have completed that show results?

Results demonstrate skills. One of the reasons personnel departments require so many credentials and tests of new employees is that they don't know how to measure your skills. As James Fallows pointed out in "The Case Against Credentialism," an *Atlantic Monthly* article, the reason blacks in this country have excelled at the performing arts and athletics is that these areas require skill, not credentials. A degree from the Harvard Business School won't get you a job with the L.A. Raiders. Skill and demonstrated results on the playing field will.

Unfortunately, business operates or fails to operate because we are a paper-crazy, class-snobbish society. If actual skill were measured in business instead of credentials, we would have many more black CEOs. The best way around this nonsense is to develop a skill that shines as clearly as the high notes of a concert soprano. Get a project and do it well, get results, document it, and get another project. If the projects have value on the outside market, you can begin to break through the credentials ceiling.

Unwinding the Ladder-Climbing Myth

If you listen to most job-search books, you should advance, plot strategies, and fight your way to the top. To the top of what? How many tiny empires should we create? Do we all need to be emperors? Advancement for its own sake—so typical of American free enterprise—is fundamentally silly. Why would you want to advance if you are happy doing what you do? Advancing to prove to the world that you are worthwhile is not a good reason. Advancing at the expense of being a good parent or husband or wife is risky trade-off as well. Advancing because you grow out of a job and need new challenges is a worthy reason.

Yet there isn't always a place to grow into within the company. The recent downsizing and restructuring of business that has eliminated middle management has created career plateaus. This shift away from vertical ladders and power grabs is not such a bad idea. The entire ladder-climbing idea of divide, conquer, smash, steal, and burn created empires for Julius Caesar, the emperors of China, and Hitler. But can you see how silly empire building is when you try to apply it to your work environment? What if you work at the post office—is it worth it to try to become emperor of the post office? How important is it to get ahead of the next guy?

How do you get ahead without climbing a ladder? Develop skills you can sell in the market to maintain steady income at your current job or on the outside. Skills you can prove you have through results will ultimately give you more job security than fancy credentials.

To advance in this economy, think horizontally, not vertically. Here are a few suggestions:

1. Stand up to everyone who criticizes you for not getting ahead.

2. Look around you instead of up the ladder. What you will see are people you care about, hobbies you have time to explore, time to reflect, and time to use your energy in ways that are creative and fulfilling to you.

3. Do work for outsiders. Use some of the skills you identified in Chapter 2 to do consulting or free-lance work. Build a network of outsiders who appreciate what you do. If you don't feel you have developed your skills sufficiently to sell them in the market-place, join a political organization and begin doing volunteer work. Solid volunteer work for people who have cash or contacts could turn into a job offer down the road. Look for ways to demonstrate your skills. If you do creative work, volunteer to do it for an organization. If you are a manager, manage a project for a nonprofit organization. The same goes for whatever it is you are good at, whether welding, accounting, or planning menus. If you are good at it, showcase it.

4. Work hard enough at your job to keep your job. Look for ways to make an impact on the company. Fulfill all the job requirements and be alert to the signs of movement within your company. If you get a poor performance review, and you know that you are doing a good job, begin looking for another job. I've seen good productive workers get fired because they rubbed the boss the wrong way or told the truth. This happens so often that you always need to be sure your skills are marketable.

5. Be loyal to your company, but don't expect it to return the favor. Don't bury your head in the sand. Always keep your finger on the pulse of the market.

6. If you love what you are doing and are motivated to work 12 hours a day at it, go for it. But if you find yourself working 12 hours a day because the culture of the organization expects it, and you don't love putting in all those hours, look for a job that is more reasonable. By not defining yourself by what you do, you begin to define yourself by what you enjoy doing. Throw your energy into what you like.

Finally, enjoy the process of working. Achievement that allows you to be marketable comes not from waiting for a magic day when everything will pay off, but by enjoying where you are every day.

VGM CAREER BOOKS/CAREERS FOR YOU

VGM Career Horizons

a division of *NTC Publishing Group*
4255 West Touhy Avenue
Lincolnwood, Illinois 60646-1975